Facebook Marketing

Strategies for Advertising, Business, Making Money and Making Passive Income

Written By Noah Hope

Table of Contents

Introduction

Thank you for downloading the book, *"Facebook Marketing."* The fact you've taken an interest in how marketing on Facebook can work for your business means you're already aware of the power of this online platform. That's half the battle. Now all you need is a few tools to start building your business's muscle, using this massively popular online social networking platform.

The internet has reformed most of the existing aspects of our economies and everyday life, but it has also ushered in some wholly new concepts. Furthermore, the emergence of social media and networks as one of the leading forms of communication between people, no matter how distant, has taken these changes to a whole new level. Needless to say, the ease with which we now communicate thanks to social media has tremendous potential which stretches far beyond chatting and personal messaging. Communication has been the driving force of progress since the dawn of mankind, and its sophistication in this era changes absolutely everything.

Marketing is no exception to this revolutionary wave of changes. Social media, Facebook above all, is a never before seen spring of crucial information regarding the market. It is a platform where you can take a peek into the way people think and into the things they seek. Any business offering a service or product to potential clientele must focus their attention on the activities of users on social media if they are to improve and grow.

As you may or may not know, a total of over one and a half billion users worldwide actively make use of Facebook every month. The marketing potential of this network is not merely in that number, though, it is much more than that. Facebook is a goldmine of valuable personal information that can be used to devise the most effective marketing strategies and achieve maximum impact on your targeted demographic or group. Its unprecedented prevalence, as well as the highly personalized nature of the way people use it, make Facebook a platform that has all but revolutionized advertising.

This book contains proven steps and strategies about how to promote your business, gain a wider client base and increase your sales by using Facebook as an online marketing platform. You'll find out to get so much more from Facebook's unique features than you are now. You'll also be given the opportunity to re-examine your general marketing strategy from the standpoint of brand identity and how you can sharpen it and make it more effective, using Facebook.

Millions of people use Facebook every day. In your hometown alone, almost everyone under the age of 30 has a Facebook page. A whopping 57% of millennials use Facebook daily. If you are planning on starting a business, or if you already have one, it's essential to use this platform to promote your business for these reasons. Facebook has become increasingly popular, growing well beyond the demographic that was originally responsible for its exponential growth. Even your mom uses Facebook these days!

This book will help you build your Facebook assets, create followers, and convert them into customers who will buy your products or services.

This book will prevent you from spending too much time using trial-and-error methods. It will provide you with tested methods to make sure you're successful with even your maiden Facebook marketing campaign.

Thanks again for downloading this book, I hope you enjoy it!

Chapter 1: Facebook Marketing – How it's Shaping Businesses

Traditional advertising, while still in play, is considered much less effective due to the general absence of necessary data about consumers. Consumer data helps promoters know if a marketing campaign is successful or not. When advertising on TV stations, for example, marketers get only a vague idea of the number of people they're able to reach. The data TV advertising sales teams is showing clients is already stale by the time clients see it. This is especially true nowadays, as the internet bites into the traditional television advertising market. The same goes for radio stations and print publications.

Another shortcoming with traditional marketing methods is the accuracy, or lack thereof, with which the adverts are implemented. Namely, billboards, TV, newspapers and similar ads work on an almost "spray and pray" principle. There aren't many sure ways to know not only the number of people who will see your adverts but the kind of people you are marketing your product to as well. Minding the latter is incredibly important if your strategies are to produce considerable results. The more you know about your targeted market, the more effective your ads can be. Facebook marketing allows you to tap into specific communities of people, who have particular interests and whose desires and interests can be identified. This means that your advertising efforts can be tailored and modified to cater to certain groups of people, with the chances of your adverts falling on uninterested ears and eyes being brought down to a minimum.

Instead of building your advertising effort on a vague idea of what people may or may not be interested in, and then hoping they stop to listen or take a look at your products and services, Facebook marketing allows you to lay down a much more solid foundation. This foundation will be strengthened by concrete knowledge and insight into the interests, wishes, mental processes, and trends that are present among your audience. In advertising, this information is the alpha and omega of success.

Internet marketing has evolved over the years. Online ads started by showing banners similar to what we see in newspapers and magazines. With the emergence of YouTube and other video hosting websites, the ability to promote products and services also expanded. Since the 1990's, online marketing enthusiasts, online-based companies and online business owners have been improving the way they promote their products and services to internet users.

These early stages of online marketing still suffered from the problems traditionally associated with advertising. The advertisers put up their material in a weakly informed fashion, just hoping for the best. This began to change rapidly in the modern digital era, and the information that would direct online marketing campaigns towards success became more and more available to businesses. Although Facebook is right there at the top when it comes to efficient online marketing, it was arguably Google that heralded the real revolution.

Google is one of the frontrunners in the world of internet marketing. They have services specifically designed for advertisers and ad publishers. Google revolutionized online marketing by providing a vast array of data to their clients. Advertisers and advertising publishers no longer operated blindly. They now had a world of data at their fingertips to help them improve performance.

Users will thus encounter ads which are selected and strategically placed based on their browsing habits. It doesn't take much experience or expertise in advertising to see the value of this system. None of your efforts will go to waste when your ads target and land exclusively on the exact people you want to market to. Advertising is all about efficiency after all, especially paid advertising. You don't want to invest into a marketing strategy that doesn't work, obviously, but it isn't just about the fact that you won't get an increase in sales. An even bigger danger lies in the fact that poor advertising choices can also cause damage to your brand and your name, thus setting your business back even further.

What is Facebook Marketing and Why is it Effective?

Facebook marketing builds on what its predecessors and competition started. Facebook provides advertisers with "insights" or statistical information. Aside from that, Facebook has many other special features that no other online advertising platforms have. One of these features is having a clearly defined goal. In most advertising platforms, you can only count views, clicks or visits to your website or your page. Using Facebook, you can count other metrics, like page likes, social engagement, and specific call-to-action success rates.

Why Use Facebook to Promote your Business?

What separates Facebook marketing from the pack is the social aspect. With Google, as with traditional advertising, advertisers have no idea of the specific reactions of people to their ads. They only know the success rate of their ads in terms of converting people to making a purchase, but they do not have insights about what's happening in between.

This is where the mental processes of the potential buyer are taking place and, thanks to Facebook, can be observed and analyzed. If an advert fails to increase sales, this is where you will be able to see how people reacted and why your approach is not delivering the desired results. And if your marketing strategy is successful, on the other hand, you will be granted insight into the causes of that success as well, helping you build on that and further develop your system for even better effect.

This has always been one of the most difficult aspects of traditional marketing. Online marketing has brought with it a whole new world of precision analytics that have opened the door to a rich field of data that allows you to continually tweak your messaging and customer approach. God is in the details and online marketing is all about little details that tell you where you need to tweak, pull in your horns, or put your foot to the floor (as the case may be).

- You can see people's responses to your marketing strategies.

On Facebook, many of your marketing tools are in the form of content. People interact with your business and brand through the content you share. Most brands disguise their ads to look like regular, non-commercial content. This gives the ads an authentic feel when people view them. Content of this type also feels friendlier and less threatening than full on commercial appeals. While the appeal is still there and you still want the sale, you're taking a less aggressive approach that takes into account buyer sensitivity to advertising overload. This helps you develop a relationship with your audience, and while traditional business falls short, data wise, it's 100% right about the importance of relationships. The sale doesn't happen without the relationship, even if the only relationship is with your product or services.

When you upload different types of content to your Facebook page, you will be able to gauge the level of success of each, based on people's reactions to what you share. Depending on what these reactions tell you, you can make changes in some parts of your strategy and retain others.

Most people will like a post that they enjoyed, which is a direct indication of a positive reaction most of the time. Then there are comments, which are significantly less numerous than likes, but a certain percentage of people will still comment on various content and usually give an even more detailed piece of feedback. More recently, Facebook introduced yet another way for users to give their five cents on a post or content, and that's reactions. People can now choose from a few available reactions and express joy, love, anger, sadness or shock. Obviously, this allows people to be even more expressive and do so in a quick and easy manner, but this is also a very useful tool to study your market and observe the effectiveness of the strategies you are implementing.

- Better audience targeting

Internet marketing is overtaking traditional forms of advertising because online advertisers have access to people's personal information. Google's ad placing algorithm, for example, shows you ads based on your internet behavior in the past. It knows the types of websites you visit. This gives Google a glimpse into your age, gender, preferences, interests and hobbies. It basically means they know what you like and they will adjust the types of ads they show you based on this information.

Facebook has enhanced this area of online advertising data because people create profiles within the platform. A person's profile contains all the information Google tries to extrapolate by examining your online habits. The Facebook ad mechanism doesn't need to makes guesses about your personal information, because you willingly give it to them by completing and updating your profile.

Who would have known, back in the pre-internet days of traditional marketing, that people can simply be asked to give out such information? It's not that simple now either, but it is very simple nonetheless. Users are offered a useful service by Facebook; their connection and communication with friends and family as well as communities they are interested in are more facilitated than ever. In return, users fill their profiles with personal information, which is useful for many reasons. And, of course, none of it is mandatory, people voluntarily put up this information – they are even happy to do so.

The nature of Facebook is such that almost all samples are fully authentic. Facebook has systems in place to prevent fake profiles, pseudonyms, etc. People use the site under their real name, and they conduct themselves under that name throughout the site. This means that there is much less room for trolling and scamming, which makes the information on the site genuine and much more useful than what is found on the majority of other social networks.

For instance, Facebook has more than one way of determining your location. If the user is using a mobile device, Facebook can ask the user to turn on his device's geolocation features. The app can also use the IP address of the user to determine his location. Also, the user generally provides information about where he currently lives. This is the third layer of information that can help the app decide where you are located.

This helps to automatically filter out that bulk of users which happens to be beyond the reach of your business. Such a system is universally beneficial. The users of the website will rarely, if ever, be exposed to pointless adverts which don't relate to them whatsoever, and your business' advertising efforts will be as accurate as possible, directed only at buyers of utmost potential. You won't have to worry about where your ads show up and whether they are reaching the right audience, you will only have to mind the quality of your campaign and focus on your creativity, Facebook will do the rest and make sure the ads land where they are supposed to.

By filling out your profile, you provide Facebook with a rich mine of data concerning your demographic markers. What you share, like and comment on, adds another layer of information. The depth of data available on Facebook about its users is incredibly useful to businesses hoping to tap into knowledge of their target markets and what those markets need, want and will buy.

Chapter 2: Building an Online Community with Facebook

Facebook is not only an advertising publishing platform. If you're only utility for promoting your business on Facebook is to create ads linked to your sales page, then you are greatly underutilizing the platform.

One of the best ways to become successful at building your Facebook presence is by creating an online community with your customers as the members. There are multiple ways in which you can start doing this and there are many ways for you to measure a person's level of participation in your community.

What you want is an interactive platform where each follower feels like they are part of the community. Your Facebook page is so much more than just a place for you to push out ads and hope that people pay attention to them – because they probably won't.

It's simple if you think about it. Why would people like a page just to get ads in their feed? Most people already look to avoid ads online as much as possible. There's hardly a person alive who would willingly just look at ads for no reason. So, you can and should do a lot more with your community on Facebook. Make it a fun place that gives people a reason to dedicate room in their feeds to your content. Let them post their own things, hold contests, and do giveaways. Make people laugh, give them valuable information and trivia, make your page worth their time and there will be plenty of room to advertise your products in there.

1. Make your target audience aware that you are on Facebook.

This can be done in a number of ways. If you have a newsletter that a lot of your customers have subscribed to, then simply let them know that you have created a Facebook page and that you would like them to check it out and follow you there. Tell them about the nature of the page and about the content that you post there, as well as any potential contests and giveaways. Your page will also be an effective means of contact that people can use to ask questions about your products and services.

Furthermore, if your business has a website or anything similar, make sure that you link your Facebook page on there for everyone to see. As always, be careful not to become annoying, but definitely make sure that everyone can see that you have a Facebook page.

If you've been making all the right moves with your company and you have a basic awareness of advertising and marketing your product or service, you'll understand the words "brand awareness".

Brand awareness is what happens when you spread the gospel of whatever product or service it is you're in the business of selling. People know you're there, what you've got and why they might like to buy it. But brand awareness is a way of thinking about your business that goes well beyond quality. Of course you're selling a quality service or product, but what's the texture of your brand? What's the color? Who are you talking to and what is it that triggers their decision that they want what you've got?

A successful brand keeps certain principles, an identity, and an aura of personality about it. When people think or talk about your brand, they need to connect particular notions to your brand name. You want these notions to be quality goods and services, excellent customer service, friendliness, charitableness, etc. A brand that has a personality will stick with the customers, and it will be harder for them to forget and replace you with the competition.

Being aware of your own brand is the start of making others aware of it and wanting to get some of what it represents. This awareness of your brand will also help you pinpoint who your followers should be on Facebook and how likely they are to become your clients.

It all boils down to the old "know yourself" wisdom. If you lack a concrete idea of what your business is and where you want to take it in the future, there is hardly a way for you to represent and promote it effectively, is there? Brands are a lot like people. Those who are self-aware and in touch with both their strengths and weaknesses, as well as those who know where they are headed and what they want, will show confidence and stability.

Knowing Your Market

Whatever it is you're selling, you need to know who's most likely to buy it. Have you done your homework? Whether it's widgets, hamburgers or acrylic nails, you need to know who your brand is targeted to. That means, essentially, who is most likely to buy what your brand represents.

Sometimes, doing some research if you lack the in-depth knowledge of the market you're aiming for can go a long way towards improving the impact of your marketing strategy. Make sure that you can identify demand for your products and services. Find out if people really need what you are selling and why they need it. Inventing need and convincing people that they should buy something that isn't really necessary to have has been successful but a few times in history. It's always best and more feasible to just conduct a thorough analysis of the market and respond accordingly.

Some businesses are so powerful that they can actually influence the market and make people interested in something they otherwise wouldn't care about. This rarely happens, though, and you are better off just adapting to the forces of the market. So, consider your product and listen to your targeted market. Some products are easier to market as their purpose and demographics of interest are fairly obvious.

Acrylic nails are a no brainer. Most people who avail themselves of this service are women and most of those women are between a certain age, a certain income level and perhaps even a of certain marital status. Knowing your market is something you should have taken the time to pin down as part of your business plan. Even if you didn't take that step and flew by the seat of your pants, you can still take a little time to gather the information you need to define the market you're selling to and figure out how to make your brand speak to that market. Striking out on Facebook, as I've said, is about data. Behind that data, though, there are people and speaking to them, person to person, is what can set you apart when marketing your business online.

So, what's your niche? What corner of the market are you hoping to carve out and service with your business?

Who are you Talking to and Where are They?

Defining your market is about asking the right questions. Where do the people you're hoping to sell to live? Where do they work? Having a clear idea of who your potential customers are helps you find them and connect.

The smaller the niche, the more effective you will be in connecting with your targets and also, communicating with them. Certain niches are more tight-knit than others as the number of people who share an interest in them is limited. These are usually much more connected and forming a community within such niches is easier. Therefore, the relationship you build with your customers and followers is likely to be a more personal and committed one.

When you establish a strong relationship with the customers, a certain degree of trust goes into it, and you will take on certain responsibilities. The chances are that people will really care about the niche in question, so you need to be careful with how you conduct yourself. Establishing a popular page that concerns one of the smaller niches, for example, can gather around quite a loyal followership that will care about the quality of your content and products a great deal. It's important to be sure that you can consistently deliver quality services, products, or content, but it's also crucial to mind the integrity of your page if you happen to be managing one. What this means is not "selling out" and being careful as to what you are advertising and promoting on your page.

If you are not able to create some of the trust that your audience is looking for, you will find that you are not going to reach your goals. Those tight=knit niches may be the best for making a sale, but when you make them angry, aren't able to work with their goals and dreams, or say something that bothers them or makes them lose trust in you, it is going to be really hard to get all of that back.

There are a lot of people who are able to fit into your target niche, but you need to make sure that you are able to find them. Before you go out searching, a good idea is to sit down and write out all the demographic features that you would like to target in order to sell the product. Who are the people that would purchase your product? What do they do when they want to have fun? How old are there, what do they like to wear, who are their friends?

All of these questions are important when you are setting up your niche. You are going to be responsible for finding these people, and if you do the demographics wrong, you are not going to get the people that you want. Be careful with your goals and reaching the right demographics, and you are sure to find plenty of people who would like to purchase from your business.

The People in your Neighborhood

As you hone in on the people you want to sell to, you will find that you come to know your product or service much more intimately as part of the process. You're no longer a coffee shop. You're a "hip, urban gathering point for young professionals". What you've discovered is that your brand can be tweaked to take advantage of key demographics that buy your product or service. You may have been operating your coffee shop for years, but did you track area trends in the neighborhood in which it's located? Did you know the demographic had shifted recently and that your coffee shop needs a brand tweak?

Your brand needs to be a name associated with being trendy and in synch with the times and the popular culture of the community you are in. While that can mean slightly altering the program from time to time, you should also try and make any and all changes in your business seamless and part of a smooth transition. It's not absolutely necessary, perhaps, but changing the way you do business too often and too abruptly can annoy many customers and come across as being too fast to pander to trends, which in turn can make a business lose some respect.

If you think of Facebook as an online metropolis, defining your online clients is not unlike defining your brick-and-mortar clients, in the example of the coffee shop. What do the people in your neighborhood need and how can you speak to that need?

What do they want?

Business is a two-way conversation. You observe. You Listen. You analyze. Looking at your product or service through the lens of your customer is a best practice you need to pursue now, if you're not already. Surveys can help you understand what your customer desires, but the best possible way of knowing what your prospective clients want it to have a conversation.

If your customers and potential clients are well aware of your Facebook page and are already visiting it, for example, you can just ask away directly and find out whatever you need. You can put up polls and raise certain ideas or questions with your customer base and survey their demands and preferences that way. It's a simple form of direct conversation and feedback, and it happens to work just fine no matter how big or small your page may be.

Of course, in the case of managing a Facebook page, keep an eye on the feedback through likes, shares, reactions, and comments. Relatively often, people will write down a comment saying why they liked or didn't like something, with the latter being even more likely.

Out there in the 3D world, business people have traditionally used avenues like the local Rotary Club, the gym and volunteering as a means of having their ears to the ground. Facebook is not that different. Joining online communities that serve your demographic is an important way to keep track of what they're talking about and to gather information about what they want and need. Join the online communities they're part of. Jump into conversations. Share with them how you can answer their need and ask how you might do that more effectively.

Rubber, Meet Road

You will now have a much clearer picture of where your business and the needs of your prospective clients converge. This is where the rubber meets the road and your business becomes that special something your market wants and needs. On Facebook, it sets you apart from the herd of other operations selling similar products or services, but not like yours and not the way you're selling that product or service. That's because you are now speaking to the client's needs; the needs you've come to know by embedding yourself and your business in that client's world.

That makes your business one that can stay the course. Once you're fostered the habit of keeping your ear to the ground, it will stick with you. You'll move forward with servicing the needs of your market toward creating a solid footing in your economic niche.

Your Story

Take a look at all the elements of how you're telling the world your story. With your market in mind, review all the materials you've been using to tell the story about why your product or service is what people need and why they should buy it.

Consider every single aspect of your brand's identity and make sure they come together well to get your message across. Everything matters; your logo, statement, customer service, the colors you use, etc. If you look at the most successful brands out there, you will find that the vast majority of them have a sort of theme, if you will, consolidating their identity in the minds of the consumers. They consistently use a well-established logo, often have a catchy slogan that sticks and their color schemes become iconic over time. This isn't to say that these aspects of your brand cannot be altered and renovated at times, but it's important to be decisive and have a stable brand personality.

Is your logo telling people what they want to hear? It's a visual, but is it speaking the language of those you want to reach? Is it evocative of what you're selling? Is it evocative of the market's needs? Compare it to other logos in the market. You may like it and you may believe it's serving your needs, but your preferences and those of the client need to match. You're telling a story about what you've got to sell. How is that story going to be received? On Facebook, a logo needs to stand out, but it also needs to tell your story, while appealing to your market. While this is also true of the 3D world, Facebook is extremely visual, so your logo needs to pack a punch. It also needs to meet design standards for readability, "friendliness" and contemporary market norms. Does it need freshening up? What worked five years ago will not work today. The same is true of five years from today.

Do you have a mission statement? A slogan? I sure hope so.

A brief statement of what you hope to do with your business, or what you believe it's already doing, is a key ingredient in the branding process. It's part of what you do. It tells your story in one brief statement that can be easily digested and remembered. Whether you choose to create a longer mission statement that can be whittled down to a few words, or to select from key words, the key to creating an effective mission statement is to tell your business's story.

All the word craft and wit you can muster will come in handy here. While it may sound simple enough, you may find that it's actually hard to say so much in so few words, but you still want to keep your slogan as concise as humanly possible. People appreciate simplicity when it comes to grabbing their attention, and if you manage to do that, there will be plenty of time later to show them the ins and outs of your business and go into details of what you're all about. The slogan just needs to invite a customer and show them that you mean business. Say, for example, that you have a plumbing company. "We fix pipes at home, at the office, and we also sell tools for plumbing" is the kind of thing you want to avoid, as well as cheesy and overinflated statements of glory and boasting. Now, "Fixing pipes!" is a slogan that packs a punch, tells the customer exactly what your business is about in two simple words, and is sure to be remembered. If a potential customer wants tools to fix the pipes on their own, they will check out your store or call the office, rest assured.

While it's usually more informative, your slogan still serves a purpose that is very similar to that of your logo. Slogans usually serve to further paint the visual picture of your brand, and they almost always accompany the brand logo in most places.

On Facebook, as I said above, visuals are king. Words, while important, need to say as much as possible in as short a time as possible. People scroll through their timelines looking for items of interest. You're competing with pictures of cats, people's lunches, daily world events and selfies. How will your story hold up under that kind of competition? How will it garner the attention of your potential market?

Whatever you say, make it short and make it count. Never forget that people usually come onto Facebook to either talk to someone or kill time after a long day. They usually have neither the time nor the patience to read through long descriptions and devote a longer period of time to figuring out what your business is about. Add to that the increasingly small attention span of most people online, coupled with thousands upon thousands of distractions at every turn, and you'll quickly realize why you need to keep things concise and to the point.

Put your Toe in the Water

Your next move is to get your product or service out there. Now that you know your market and how you can answer its unique needs, do a test promotion.

There's hardly a better way to see the effect of your marketing campaign than just to do a test run and get straight into it. Choose a specific product or service that you want to test out and promote it on your Facebook page, for example, where you can get the clearest idea of what people think about it based on the detailed feedback and insights provided by Facebook. There are a few things you can do to feel the market, apart from just selling the product right away.

Offer your market something to get them interested. That could be an invitation to a grand opening (or re-opening), a sample chapter of a book, a discount coupon, or even a contest. Sometimes, if you are fairly confident in your product or service, it may be a good idea only to give the customers a taste of what you have to offer. If you see great success with the trial marketing, then eventually offering the whole thing after the positive initial response can bolster your impact on the market even further.

Facebook contests are a fun way of getting your business's name circulated and more widely known. Everybody loves a contest. Asking people to like and share a post, or to leave a comment to enter is also a way to push your page engagements and keep the contest visible to your audience. You may even want to ask people to like your page, by posting to some of those community pages mentioned above. This will widen your reach and thus, your brand awareness.

By testing your product and service in this way, you will be able to analyze market response and take your online strategy's pulse.

Brand awareness is a process. If the way you're doing things isn't working out for you, then re-brand, or re-examine your strategy. At the top of your mind is what your target market wants and needs and how your unique business can better speak to those desires. Remember, it is you who has to adapt to and satisfy the market, it is your business that has to be finely tuned and tailored to the customers' needs, not the other way around.

Reach

Reaching the audience is the cornerstone and most crucial step in any marketing endeavor. In fact, reach is what marketing is all about by definition. Luckily, we are talking about the internet and social media, which are all about reach at their very core. There are tools on Facebook specifically designed to help you extend the reach of your brand and market your goods with greater effect.

The first step in creating a Facebook community is to let the people who may need your products and services know that they've landed on Facebook and are open for online business. There are two ways to do this: organic reach and paid reach. In Facebook insights, the metric you need to look at when you want to increase awareness is referred to as "reach". How many people are seeing what you post?

- Organic Reach

Organic reach refers to the content you post on your page. These are nuggets of information your page fans may find useful or entertaining. If they enjoy your content, or if it moves them emotionally, they may press "like", add a comment, or share the information with their friends. When they do this, their personal connections will also be able to see your content. The three actions mentioned above are referred to as "engagement". When your content receives thousands to millions of engagements in a short period, this is known as "going viral".

There is no way to guarantee your content will go viral. However, you should still try to create content that increase your chances of that happening, based on your business's target audience. When people see the content you share, they'll also see your page's name. If your page's name seems interesting, people may pay it a visit. The more people see your content, the more people will know about your brand and the more potential you'll have to increase your sales.

Again, this is the part where the importance of your brand's image comes to light. Your logo, slogan, page title, etc. all come together into play here. Your content may be good quality, and people may enjoy it, but if the way you present your page and brand is uninteresting and unappealing, the chances are that the user won't go any further in seeing what your business is all about. This is especially true for those users who got to your content by having it shared to them by friends and other contacts on Facebook.

Think about it. If a friend sends you a funny picture, video, or any similar type of content, even if you liked it a lot, how often do you actually go to the source page and inspect it further? Many people usually don't do that; they just chuckle at the picture, move on, and continue about their day. This is why you want your page to be represented in a way that instantly attracts people to check it out and in a way that makes people want to come back for more.

What's more, some users share content, particularly images, in full screen on their browser. For you, this means that the source of the content (your page) will not be named or shown anywhere; the user will only see the image and have no idea of where it comes from. Now, if your page is very interesting, those who share your content may even recommend to their friends that they go take a look at your page.

Another way to encourage users to share the actual link, still within the confines of your page, is to make your image content work together with the textual description to the side of it. If a picture needs its description to be funny or make sense, users will, of course, share the whole thing. This way, when the user is looking at the content, your page will be explicitly represented just to the right of the content they are enjoying, prompting them to check it out.

Reputation, Community and Reach

Your business's profile in the community depends on a lot of factors and one of the most important is reputation. While this is always dependent on the quality of your product or service, it also depends on perception and visibility.

How your immediate community (where you do business, in your city, town, or region) sees you is of primary concern for any business. Being present to the community as more than a business; as a civically-minded, charitable and engaged members of that community is very important for this reason.

While networking with other area business is important, it's also crucial that your business be involved in the immediate community. Perhaps entering a local run for charity, or an annual parade, or offering prizes for fundraising events would benefit not only you, but the community. When your business's name is front and center at local events in these and other ways, your profile grows and your respect quotient does too.

If your budget allows it, you can also host events simply for the entertainment of the community. People love to have fun, especially if there is competition and a chance to win something involved. Such events are a great way of promoting your business and building a reputation, but they are also an opportunity to let people try out your products and services, which they will gladly do.

This extends to Facebook. While you're in the business of promoting your goods or services, you're also part of a community, with events, charities and other local businesses. Your posting should reflect this reality as often as possible. People like to hear about themselves and where they live, so posting about events with a high profile in your community is another important means of reaching out to your local market.

National holidays and special days like Christmas should also be on your posting schedule. It's almost unthinkable that any business would have the poor taste to forget about significant events, in the world of Facebook. Making a point of posting a Memorial Day greeting to thank veterans, or a Fourth of July message is an indication of your humanity and sense of connection to something greater than yourself and your business.

Posting about occasions like these and others also provides you with an opportunity to leaven and freshen your content and to keep it interesting. Posting an endless litany of the merits of your product or service can become tedious. It turns people off and that's the last thing you want!

Certain holidays and celebrations have a unique feeling about them, and they put a lot of people into a particular emotional state and frame of mind. Christmas is an old and great example of this. People rush to buy certain products during the holiday season, and they buy a lot. The advertising industry has been carefully studying people's behavior during Christmas for decades, and there have been countless strategies and marketing tactics devised to make good use of the holidays to bolster sales.

This isn't to say that you have to be cold and calculating all the time, always looking to exploit everything to improve business, but it's definitely paramount that you keep track of these social tides. Promote a unique, season-specific product when Christmas comes around. Come across in a friendly and sincere manner as always. Make sure that people see you are enjoying the holidays as well.

Humor is something else your page (and your brand) needs. Everyone loves a joke. Puns, funny pictures (especially those which relate – even obliquely – to your business) is another source of viable content. It gives you and your brand a human face, creating instant reliability.

- Paid Reach

Aside from posting organic content, you can also increase awareness by paying for Facebook ads. When creating a Facebook ad, you'll be asked for the goal of your ad campaign. It's not advisable to pay for ads just to increase your reach. Just by creating a campaign with any type of goal, you will already increase your reach. For this reason, you need to save your advertising money for goals with more observable outcomes.

It is a good idea to wait until you have reached a certain level of popularity with your page. It may be difficult to do at times, without the paid advertisements, but it certainly can be done. Once you have a considerable followership and a successful Facebook page, you will have a clearer idea of where you want to go from there and how exactly you want to shape your brand on the market. This is when financial investment into your campaign begins to be a much more useful and cost-effective method.

Paid ads vary in a wide range of prices and arrangements, and you will find that some are very affordable. When you do decide you want to start paying for ads, you may want to start small and see how the cheaper options fare on your market first, before going further.

- Off-Facebook methods

It is also advisable to put call-to-action statements such as "like us on Facebook" on all your marketing materials. If you have a brick and mortar store, you should put the Facebook sign there. You can also train your store cashier to encourage people to visit your Facebook page.

If you own a restaurant, for example, you can also provide free Wi-Fi so that people can easily share photos of the food you serve to their pages. You can also put the call-to-action statements on company properties. You can have these painted on the side of the building. You can have it embroidered on company uniforms and even include it in your business cards and business's website.

While this guidebook is going to take time to look at the best methods to use when marketing on Facebook, there are a lot of other marketing materials that you are using to reach your customers. Not all of your customers are going to be on Facebook and some of them may not even realize that you have a Facebook page that they should be checking out.

And this is why you should make sure that your Facebook information is present on some of your other marketing tools. Facebook is one of the easiest and most efficient ways to reach your customers and share some of the latest news and information with them. This means that you will need to make sure that your customers who don't know about your Facebook page so that they can go and visit.

Now you need to make sure that your customers are able to find you on Facebook. Consider putting the Facebook URL of your page on your business cards, on some brochures and magazines, or any other print marketing tools that you are using. This makes it easier for the customer to not only know about your Facebook page, but to also have the chance to refer back to the material later on.

1. Get Likes

After making people aware your company exists, you need to convert them from just being viewers to become active subscribers to the content you post. On Facebook, you can do this by getting people's "likes". By pressing the like button on your page, the user is basically saying to Facebook: "I want to follow this page". That person then becomes one of your "fans" or "followers". Every time you post a type of content, your online fans see them based on Facebook's newsfeeds algorithm. You can use the tips above (organic, paid and off-Facebook methods) to encourage people to like your page.

If getting page likes is your goal, then you need to make sure you're sharing content that is appealing to your target audience. More specifically, you need to post the type of content that will encourage engagement (press like, add comments and share to their friends). If your content can compel your followers to perform these actions, your page will become popular in their circles.

You can also increase page likes by using Facebook ads. This is useful for new businesses that are just starting out in the community. You instantly get an audience of people from the demographics and locations that you select on your ad properties.

Liking client pages, or the pages of prospective clients will usually earn your page a like in return. You can also send invitations to people in your network to like your page. This is somewhat effective, but targeting only those you believe will be truly interest in what you're offering will increase your chances of likes from your invitees. Being aware of your market is the foundation for finding others that may want your product or service, also and will further diffuse your brand. The old saying "you can't have too many friends" certainly rings true on Facebook. The more people who see your business's name, the more likely you are to increase your clientele. That's how brand awareness works in the real world and Facebook is no exception.

2. Post engaging content regularly

Once you have a sizable following, your next goal is to make sure they engage with your content. As mentioned above, this will help diffuse your brand.

There are four types of content you can share: text, images, videos and links. Regardless of the type of content you post, your goal is the same - to make people react through Facebook engagements.

3. Plan for long-term staying power

You need to post regularly to make sure people don't forget about your page. Facebook has many distractions. People usually visit Facebook to escape the stresses of daily life. As a Facebook page owner, you are competing with other pages for the attention of your followers. If you don't post regularly, your followers will forget you're there. Out of sight, out of mind. You will get fewer engagements and the activity in your page will slowly decrease until there are no more new visitors liking and visiting your page.

If you play it right, you will slowly create loyal followers for your brand. This will allow you to become a significant page in your market,

4. Create a group for your special customers

Customers love it when they feel special and important. You can increase your customer loyalty by giving customers special privileges that your other followers don't have. You can do this by creating a closed group where you post special types of content that your customers will find useful. This may include new promotions and opportunities. Some stores also run exclusive promotions for loyal Facebook fans.

People who are not members of the group will want to join, if your offers are enticing.

5. Convert engaged users into business customers

You do not want your Facebook page to seem salesy. If your followers are loyal however, they will sometimes forgive you if you post promotional content. They may also forgive you if you put an engaging photo or image with your promotional content. As stated earlier in the book, the trick is to make your promotions look like a regular Facebook content. This way, people can engage with it as they would with all the other content in their newsfeed. This type of content is said to be "native". Eliciting an emotional response through the use of humor, adorable animals, or even a motivational or inspirational quote can engage people much more readily than a standard commercial appeal.

Traditional advertising practices suggest your ads need to stand out from all the others competing for people's attention. This is why you see giant "SALE" signs in malls and in newspapers. These types of images do not work well on

Facebook. Unless your content is extremely good, people will be annoyed with you for disturbing their leisurely Facebook browsing with annoying, over-the-top ads. Don't get me wrong; you still need to use photos and videos that grab the attention of your fans. However, you need to make your content stand out without being an endless, monotonous sales pitch.

Avoid "Unlikes" and "Unfollows"

Facebook gives its users the option of unliking certain pages and content. Most users will not unlike your page if you give them no reason to, but there's always a reason behind follower actions. They may unlike your page because they don't like the types of posts you share. They may also do this because they are clearing the clutter from their pages. Sometimes, though, they just remove their pages. There is no point dwelling on why some people unlike your page, while others don't, because you'll probably never know.

You need to reassess the type of posts you share only in the event that more than 5% of your fans have unliked your page within the space a week or a month. To avoid these types of actions by your followers, you need to make sure you limit your posts to the type of content your target audience enjoys.

Big No-Nos

There are some cardinal rules about content you should always keep in mind, when posting to your business's Facebook page.

The first is this: it's not your personal page.

That means there are certain types of content that should never be shared. Commentary about politics, religion and sex (the Big Three, if you will) should be scrupulously avoided. Stating your political opinions is a recipe for disaster. You may know your market well, but unless you've been picking people's brains about their voting habits, you probably don't know what their political views are. It's a minefield, so stay out of it.

Religion, also, is a hot button topic of conversation that few are able to engage in without becoming heated. Discussion of religious topics must also be avoided for this reason.

While most people like sex and it's true that "sex sells", posting content of an overtly sexual nature can be offensive for some. They don't want to see it on their News Feeds. While most won't lose any sleep over it, some will and alienating your market, even a small corner of it, is not the effect you're going for. Avoid all references, criticism of and even support for alternatives sexualities, also. These topics are not for a business Facebook page. They may give satisfaction to some, or even most of your market, but if you alienate even one, news of that alienation will travel.

Alienating language should also be avoided. Using words which some are sensitive to should be avoided, at all costs. Profanity and epithets have no place on your Facebook page. Many are sensitive to this kind of language and employing it is bad practice on Facebook and in life, generally.

Everyone has opinions, but expressing them on your business Facebook page is not going to grow your market so you can move what you're selling. Keep your opinions to yourself.

If there's one thing Facebook's well known for, it's the ease with which some of its users share their opinions. An opinion expressed online seems to flow out of people's minds, through their finger tips and onto Facebook much more easily than it does in the 3D world. Followers who pick fights, raise topics like those listed above, or harass other followers are known in the online world as "trolls". Have no mercy. Block them. You're not alienating a customer by doing this. You're heading off the potential alienation of your real clients. Trolling on your page can lead to the loss of existing and potential customers.

Your Facebook page represents your business, so keeping it free of potential conflict is *de rigeur*. But have you considered how some respond to poor spelling and grammar? Many find it intensely irritating and will go as far as to unlike your page to spare themselves seeing it. While you may not think so, it's extremely important that you proof your content to ensure that it's grammatically sound, correctly spelled and engaging to read. Take the time. It's worth it.

Chapter 3: Facebook Tools and Features for Marketing

Facebook provides you with many tools that allow you to maximize the effectiveness of your marketing campaign. Here are some of them:

Your Facebook Page

There are community and business pages on Facebook that boast hundreds of thousands or even millions of likes and followers. These pages vary in their nature and goals, but among them are many prominent brand names. The Facebook pages of those brands serve well as platforms for feedback, contact, customer service, and, of course, advertising and promotions of products. Third party advertising is also not uncommon on the pages of various brands, which means the promotion of services and products offered by other businesses, usually smaller ones and affiliates.

Facebook allows every business to create a Facebook page in the network. This is a page where you post all the content that your brand's fans and followers may find interesting. If people want to keep in touch with your business through Facebook, they do it through your page. They can send you a message and share their own content to your page if you allow them to.

Before you even think about content, make sure the basic framework of your page is in place and solid. That means choosing an engaging profile avatar (this should probably be the logo that reflects your brand and speaks to your market). Your cover photo should also be readily identifiable as your brand and its texture and flavor.

The picture or logo that will represent you is important because it will be the first thing people will remember. It is, therefore, so much more than just a gimmick or an aesthetic choice. Your logo will be the visual representation of all that is your business. When people think about your brand, that logo will be the first thing to pop into their thoughts. Eventually, the logo effectively becomes your brand. This is why it's important to come up with a proper one and be consistent in using it.

It's advisable to keep the profile picture static. Constant changes to this will result in confusion and your followers may not "recognize" you immediately when you post comments on other pages, if it's changing all the time. Your cover photo can change, but only occasionally and only with the intent of leaving it in place for a very special occasion (like a promotion). A lot of Facebook success has to do with the establishment of your brand online and immediate recognition.

When it comes to the creation or selection of the logo or profile picture itself, there is hardly a universal formula of creating the perfect one. Most of the time, this will depend on the specifics and the nature of your business. You should know best what accurately represents your company, and if you are still unsure, you can always consult professionals in this regard. Just keep in mind that the profile picture of your page will show up everywhere and will often be the first thing people see and is more likely to be remembered than even the very name of your business. The picture should make clever use of colors and shapes to attract attention and stick with the viewer.

Make sure to include as much information about your business in the section provided, when setting up your page. People want to know how they can call and email. They also want to know your physical address (if there is one) and where they can find you on other platforms like Twitter, LinkedIn and Instagram or Pinterest. Be sure to be as detailed as possible.

Apart from contact information, Facebook allows you to give a good description of your business on the page as well. You can keep this concise and to the point, or you can go into greater detail if you so desire. It may be a good idea to keep it short, though, as people are very eager to move on when they are browsing through their Facebook.

Insights

When you reach 30 likes, Facebook will provide you with insights or statistics about your followers, their quantified engagement to your content, and the demographics of people following your page.

This feature enables you to see how post engagement (likes, comments, shares) compares from week to week and the percentage by which this increases or decreases. The information can help you understand the viewing habits of your followers and target these more effectively by posting appealing content.

As you will find when you get accustomed to using Facebook insights, the performance of the content you post can be impacted by the time of day or season you choose to post said content. It's not just about the content itself, its quality, or its subject matter. People are more likely to find or even enjoy certain content at a particular time. Some content may be more appropriate and better received on Monday, for example, whereas other stuff could be perfect to post just as weekend approaches. By keeping constant track of the information provided by Facebook Insights, you will pick up on this soon enough.

General statistics for your page are shown, but insights are also broken down by post, allowing you to review how your followers responded to the content you posted. This is extremely useful for discerning which content received the most positive response and also, for directing your content choices, in future.

As your page grows further, you will begin to see patterns and trends among your audience as well. Sometimes you'll have to adhere to those trends and tailor your content output to fit them better. If this means rearranging some of your posts or even letting go of certain content, then so be it. The market will always tell you what needs to be done in the end, and Facebook's insights will go a long way towards getting this knowledge.

Page Comparison

When your page reaches 100 likes, Facebook allows you to pick five other pages to compare your own page's performance to. By keeping an eye on what other pages in the same industry are doing, you will be able to know what types of content work well with your chosen audience. You can then create similar types of content to what's on offer at your competitor pages. This will help you see similar results.

Who knows, you may even catch a glimpse of what the competition is doing wrong, thus gaining an edge on them. You may see a good idea being implemented poorly on their page, an idea that can be improved and done just right with your personal touch. Like in any other business, keeping a close eye on the competitors is one of the cornerstones of success. Don't try to imitate others, though, always strive to sprinkle each approach with your own personality, or that of your brand, even if you are directly borrowing some ideas and concepts.

Facebook Business Manager

You can also opt to manage your account in the business manager view. This feature allows page managers to easily transition between pages and ad campaign views. This strategy works best if you are planning to run multiple ads on the different pages you manage.

It's also possible to gather around other users and give them special permissions to help you manage your pages and ads for you. If you have a considerable following of people, and if they enjoy your content very much and are loyal to the page, you may find that a lot of users will do this willingly and without asking for compensation. Running and managing multiple pages can be a cumbersome endeavor, so it's not a bad idea to make use of this tool to get help as well.

Call-to-action Button

Facebook also allows pages to place a call-to-action button opposite the profile picture and page title. For e-commerce websites, there is a "shop now" call to action button. If page visitors click on the button, then they will be directed to the page you've linked it to. You can edit this at any time. There are other forms of actions you can choose from based on your marketing goals, including promoting your call to action directly to your news feed.

Scheduled Publishing Option

Timing is an important factor in the success of both organic and paid campaigns. You can time your posts effectively by using the scheduled posts tab in the publishing tools of your page manager dashboard. This feature allows you to post contents at times you're not available to be online. It also allows you to post days and weeks into the future so that you won't forget to post to your followers on holidays and special occasions. As they say, timing is everything. Posting immediately before 9:00 am may not be possible for you, but with this feature, you can schedule a post to appear at that time (prime time for social media).

Scheduling your posts basically allows you to put your page on an autopilot of sorts. Not only does it come in handy when you know you will be unavailable, but it also lets you manage your time better and organize in a way that allows more free time for other activities. If you already have a clear idea of the way you want to do something in the future, why not just do it right away, schedule it to get posted at a given time, and then focus on other tasks at hand or leisure?

Chapter 4: Content Marketing in Facebook

I'm sure you know by now, but besides ease of communication with friends and family, Facebook offers a platform for sharing various kinds of content. The content on Facebook also serves a variety of purposes. People share things with the aim of news reporting, exchange of information, or simply entertainment, but the content on Facebook is often used for marketing goals as well – and successfully so.

As with any platform on the web, content marketing is an effective strategy for Facebook. It is one of the best ways to get people's attention. On Facebook, there are four types of content: text, video, images and links. Before preparing any type of content, you should become familiar with how each type of content is shown in your newsfeeds. Let's take a look.

Pure Text Content

Text contents take up the least amount of space and are probably the least engaging of the four types of content mentioned above. Facebook feeds are very busy. There are many other elements in various feeds much more likely to grab your target user's attention than pure text. The only types of text contents that consistently get attention are rants and emotional statements and these are not what you're interested in.

By large, people prefer to look at images or watch videos. For the average user, there is a lot of content to shuffle through when they visit their Facebook homepage. Upon seeing a post with a lot of text and no image or video, most people will only read the first sentence or two (if even that) before scrolling further down. On its own, textual content will work if it's exceptionally interesting or concise and grabs the reader's attention right away. Otherwise, it is important to combine it with something else that will attract the average user.

When a person sees an interesting image or video on Facebook, they are much more likely to read the text that accompanies it, so make sure that it relates and offers valuable background information on what they just saw.

Using text effectively as part of your content marketing strategy means employing economical language. It can also mean telling a story. As always, humor appeals to Facebook users, especially when combined with a unique graphic or interesting video. As a matter of fact, there's hardly a better way of reaching people than through humor. If you can make someone laugh, you can make them do all sorts of other things, least of which are sharing, liking and otherwise reacting to your content.

Whatever the story is, ensure that the punch line is arrived at soon and further, that it's supporting your brand. A customer endorsement, a success story, or promotional text should be upbeat, well-written and deliver maximum impact in as few words as possible.

Avoid the use of exclamation points as a substitute for saying something that's actually exciting. The overuse of exclamation points is a sign that you're unable to craft a message effectively. They appear unprofessional and even overwrought. Just! Say! No! to exclamation points, unless they're genuinely called for.

Just adding exclamation points into otherwise regular text is but a poor attempt to manipulate your reader's response. Unless the text has substance and really strikes a chord with the user, the chances are that they won't share your enthusiasm and will find your style of writing silly and coming across as trying too hard.

Images

Adding a compelling image is the best way to provoke engagement with your content. High quality images with positive messaging appeal to almost all users of Facebook.

The thing about images is that they are always to the point and are the most concise and impactful content you can find.

Viewing them takes a matter of seconds, and they are usually the most shared type of content out there. You'll almost always find that successful pages make frequent use of images to promote their products and punctuate their points when posting text.

Adding an image also increases your content's presence, as images command more space on the feeds of other users. As stated earlier, visual content is one of the most important features of successful feeds on Facebook and can radically improve your user engagement.

While a piece of text blends into the Facebook homepage and is easily overlooked, images immediately garner attention. It's not just about the fact that they take up more space, it's also about their power of delivering a message. If you are the creator of your visual content, try to make clever use of coloring schemes to attract attention even easier. Bright colors and adequate combinations of colors will occupy just about anybody's mind. Strong reactions to certain colors are in our very nature, and they have been used by the advertising industry for ages.

Using software to create your own images is perhaps more time-consuming than sharing existing graphics, pulled from other online sources. But taking this step is another important support for your brand. You control the imagery. You control the imagery's message and you build your brand at the same time. A bonus? You place your logo on the images you create and a message that further supports your brand. This is good practice and creating your own images is a skill you should either develop or one you might enlist someone else to do on your behalf.

Depending on the level of development of your page and your financial means, you can hire the services of illustrators and freelancers for this purpose. There are plenty of people online who are very skillful in Photoshop or Adobe Illustrator, and they make a living by producing visual content for clients. If you don't know any such people personally, you can turn to freelance websites where countless artists offer their services. Freelancer and Upwork are among such sites, and they get millions of projects assigned and done on a regular basis.

There are many rich sources for images online, one of which is Pinterest. Positive, motivational, supportive messages, for example, are very effective on Monday mornings. A message with a picture of a beach, wishing your followers a relaxing weekend might be just the ticket on a Friday. High quality images (those which are landscaped and "tabloid" size work best on Facebook) that speak to your followers are what you're looking for. There are millions out there. Use them as brand support and to boost your engagement.

Videos

Videos are the most popular of the four types of content. By uploading a video to your page, you are inviting people to enjoy a show, basically. Videos are known to boost engagement almost exponentially, particularly when they're self-produced (something you can do on your mobile device or digital camera), humorous, or based on a universal theme (peace, family, etc.).

The appeal of videos is due to a number of factors. One of those factors, again, is the fact that there is no reading to be done. Although videos require more attention than a still image, people definitely love to watch interesting ones. Videos are also a great way for people to connect as they often feature things that a lot of people have in common, making them the most relatable form of content out there probably.

The ability of Facebook videos to grab follower attention has also improved because of the auto-play feature recently implemented by Facebook. As with Instagram, the auto-play feature activates the video when you scroll onto it in your newsfeeds. Automatically, a short clip of the video posted plays without the sound.

In a moment of pure genius, someone came up with the idea of making videos play automatically on websites. This means that people will see them as they would Gif files while scrolling through their feeds. Moving pictures immediately draw people's attention much more effectively than a simple thumbnail and are very likely to make users click on them to see the full thing. Users can still disable this option on Facebook, but most of them won't bother as their playback without audio is hardly an annoyance.

Your followers will be able to see the entire video, with audio, if they click on it. During the first few months of implementation, this feature increased engagement by Facebook users exponentially and has also increased the number of videos uploaded to Facebook every day. In fact, Facebook's video engagements doubled almost overnight. The Wall Street Journal reports that 88% of top content sites on the internet now use this feature, following the success of its implementation at Facebook.

Links

Links are the only types of content that will make your followers leave Facebook. There are three parts of a link's content involved, when these are shared to Facebook. The top portion is the description (pure text content), where you can add a personal message to your followers. This is where you can put some of your humor and creativity to use to attract more attention. It's where you place your pitch and make people interested in following your link in your own words.

It's important to keep the description short and to the point, especially if the link already leads to a place where there is text to be read.

Just below it, you will see the link's preview. The preview includes a featured image and a small text area that contains the title and an excerpt of the text on the landing page. If the link leads to an article, for example, the preview will feature the title of that article, as well as the first sentence or two, giving Facebook users a glimpse into what they would read if they followed the link.

If you are trying to build an audience and get more page likes, you need to share the type of content that encourages people to take further action and follow the link you're posting. That includes offering informative text that encourages them to do so, possibly with an excerpt from the content at the link. Replacing an image from the landing page with something you feel is more evocative of the content on offer, or an entertaining video can also spur user action. Building on content in this way is great for encouraging engagement in the form of likes, shares and comments.

Remember that every single post you make and every step you take on Facebook is a new opportunity to bolster your promotional efforts and advance your relationship with the followers of the page. Approach each post as a piece of its own and give it utmost consideration as every time you post, you further consolidate your page or brand.

If your goal is to provoke certain actions by your followers, compelling them to venture outside the realm of Facebook, then you need to make effective use of links. This means supporting them with the addition of text and images that make them curious enough to take those actions.

The chances are that your followers will trust you enough to visit the links you post without thinking too much about it or being suspicious. However, there are other reasons not to visit the links posted on Facebook. Lack of interest or reason to visit the link will probably be leading cause of poor traffic. Don't underestimate the laziness of people when they are spending their leisure time browsing Facebook.

General Guidelines for Effective Facebook Content Marketing

The biggest challenge for most Facebook page managers is how to consistently create great content. If your business already has a website where you place all your content, then you only need to duplicate your actions there and perhaps customize it to appeal to your audience at Facebook.

A thing to keep in mind is that the bigger your following gets, the more content of ever increasing quality you'll need to put out to meet the demand and keep your followers interested. As your page grows, a time will come when you should begin to consider teaming up with other pages and content creators to fill up your own page with what they are producing. Having a large base is a powerful advantage that you can leverage to get more content, as smaller pages that may have good quality stuff but lack the followers will jump at the opportunity to be promoted by you.

1. Choose a goal

Before creating any form of content, you should write down your business goals for the week or the month of content marketing. Who do you want to reach? Do you want to drive traffic from Facebook to your website? If so, then see above and go beyond customization of your site's content. Offer something different for Facebook followers. Include links to key content on your web page and a call-to-action that provides your followers with a direct portal to get there.

It's also important to map out when you want to release certain content, time your posting right and form a schedule to adhere to. All good managers are highly organized and have a keen sense of timing. That's where you begin to plan out your week or month. Be considerate of any possible holidays, specific days of the week, etc. If you come up with too many goals, make use of Facebook's tools for scheduling posts to show up automatically at a given time and on a particular date.

2. Identify the type of content that you should use

Choose the appropriate types of content for the goal you've set. If you're hoping to raise brand awareness, then using a combination of imagery and video content with occasional text/link content is your best bet. What is the story you're telling and who are you telling it to? What do they want to see? These questions should be at the front of your mind when identifying the type of content that serves you best on Facebook.

Knowing your business is the first step towards representing it well. You have to know perfectly well what it is that you are doing, what you intend to do in the future, and where you want to take your enterprise. The second crucial step is knowing your market and your followers on Facebook. Marketing is a two-way street, and you won't succeed by just putting out content for the sake of putting out content. It's paramount that you constantly observe your audience and their reactions to your posts. Be mindful of what makes them laugh, sets them off, and what produces the most user engagement. Always adjust your content to the requirements of the market and be ready to reconsider the ideas you may have had before, as you may sometimes find that what you thought would cause a significant reaction was actually met dissatisfaction.

3. Produce quality content

Image-based content is easy to find online. Your goal, though, is to ensure it's of high quality and relevant to your brand's mission. Further, it must be compelling enough to engage your followers. As said above, though, creating your own image-based content is by far the more effective strategy. You are in control. Often, you'll find you need to create your own images, as you can't find quite what you're looking for elsewhere. It's worth the time and effort to brand yourself effectively and maintain control of your message.

Once again, it may be a good idea to seek professional assistance if you have the monetary means for that. Make use of someone else's proficiency in visual design software and get original, quality content tailored to your specific needs, without putting any of your own time into it. If you don't have the money but have the time, though, there are many good courses and tutorials online, paid and free, which you can use to learn these skills for yourself and produce completely original content by your own hand.

The same goes for video content. However, videos don't just require a camera; there is also editing that goes into the job, or even effects if the situation demands it. This is, again, all something that you can do on your own if you have the skills, the time, and the tools, but it may prove harder than expected. The power of today's software definitely facilitates such processes like never before, but it's still a skill to be mastered. Luckily, there are plenty of freelance editors and video creators out there who excel at such tasks and offer their services for a fixed or hourly rate. If you need animation, you can arrange that too. The only limitation is your budget. Videos are sometimes hard to make if you want quality production, though, and it is very important that they are visually appealing and smooth for the viewer.

Quality videos are more difficult to create on your own. Posting low quality or pixelated videos may hurt your page's reputation rather than improve it. But in this age of top notch mobile device technology, it's likely you're up to the challenge. Trial and error will tell you if the videos you provide yourself are going to work for you. If you have a big marketing budget, then you can have videos made for your Facebook page. You should need to ensure, however, that those videos would help you reach your Facebook marketing goals. Otherwise, all your video making efforts will be for nothing. Again, examining what competitors have done in this area is useful.

Linking your Facebook page to your website or blog is an effective way of spreading the gospel of what you're selling. Your site or blog should feature a varied content mix that's exciting to visit, because it's well maintained and not static. There's nothing worse than sending followers to your website and having them discover it hasn't been updated for weeks. This will turn them off in a hurry. Keep your content fresh and evolving. You should then share your website to Facebook by either posting the link in your page's status bar or by using your website's share-to-Facebook feature. Don't forget to include compelling text content to encourage your followers to click on the link. Driving two way traffic between Facebook and the other web presences of your brand will grow your online identity.

4. Optimize your posts for maximum engagement

Facebook allows page managers to add a short description to all the content types they share. Aside from auto-playing videos, these descriptions are probably the most attention-grabbing element of any post. People look at this factor when they become interested in viewing the video, image or link that you've share.

Users will want to know the gist of the content before deciding whether or not they want to give it a more thorough look. That's why your description needs not only to be concise, but very descriptive and easily understood. Always aim to provide as much information as possible, while keeping the number of words in the description to an absolute minimum.

You need to make sure your description uses the kind of language your target audience usually sees in their feeds. Posting questions and emotional statements in the description is also effective in gathering engagement. Humor is another useful tool for user engagement, when carefully choosing your words to introduce your content.

Funny content is likely at the very top when it comes to sharing. People just love a laugh or a chuckle, and they will make sure to share that with their friends, who may share it even further. Another type of content that generates a lot of sharing is shocking content, and I mean that in the most general sense, but these kinds of stunts should be avoided as they are more risky. You can never go wrong with a fair amount of humor, though.

Including a headline in your content is another effective strategy for catching user attention. Facebook usually posts the page titles of links when they're shared. If you're using links to direct traffic to your website, then you need to make sure you optimize the page title to encourage clicks on your links. An effective format to encourage this action is adding a word that suggests further action by the user. Examples of words like these are "click", "visit", "look", or "check out". Take a look at the call-to-action words your competitor pages use. What's working there? What's not? Encouraging engagement with the use of language that invites an interactive relationship with your users can be a very effective means of boosting your presence. It also brings users into a two way communication with you and your brand. You invite. They take up the invitation.

It may sound overly simplistic and too direct to yield a result, but it usually does work. A word as simple as "click" urges immediate action and can be surprisingly impactful. Sometimes the simplest way to make someone do something is just to ask them to, and the internet is full of examples where this simple principle happens to work.

You can also add a headline to images and videos. For images, you can do this by adding text at the top of the image, using image manipulation software like Photoshop or GIMP. This strategy works well with videos, because the auto-play features doesn't provide audio, as we discussed earlier.

Measure Effectiveness

If your content is fully optimized to help you reach your goals, then you need to find a way to measure its effectiveness. Some goals can be measured using the insights feature of the Facebook page. If your goal includes actions outside the network, you may need to use data gathering tools like Google Analytics to measure your campaign's success.

As we will discuss a little later on in this book, Facebook offers a few tools to help you monitor the impact of your marketing campaign. You can track all kinds of actions like clicks, likes, views, registrations, checkouts, shares, etc. These tools can be used to get deeper insight into the efficiency of both your Facebook page and your other websites that you manage and promote over Facebook ads.

- Experiment with possible improvements

No marketing campaign is perfect. There are always some areas in need of improvement. The best features of your content and ad campaigns will change as your page audience and your marketing goals change. Experiment with your strategy, tweaking as you go. The online world is dynamic and volatile. You need to remain sensitive to that and nimble enough to shift your focus.

Your targeted market is a living, breathing thing that reacts to many different forces like trends and new social climates, and your page or site will need some work until it becomes influential. Regardless of your influence, the market will always tell you what you are doing right and what needs to change. You just have to read the signs and pay attention, while always ready to change habits and alter your approach as the people demand.

Chapter 5: Maximize the Use of Facebook's Niche Communities

Page managers should always consider how they can leverage their networks on Facebook to make each ad campaign more successful. Here are some ways to achieve this:

- Take note of what other people in your niche like to share

What type of content gets the greatest user engagement and reach? Try to break the properties of this content down and look for ways in which you can duplicate or approximate that content's success in your own niche.

This also means paying attention to trends, which are really the driving force of all social media. Always be mindful of what other successful pages are doing and what is bringing in the views, likes and shares. These trends change all the time and very frequently too, as interests and focus of the user base shift rapidly on the internet. Trends always provide a lot of potential to tap into new markets, sell your products and services, as well as expand your base.

- Communicate with other page managers

You should build a personal network of Facebook page managers. Look at your friends list on Facebook and check who among your connections manages a page successfully.

You can meet them and arrange to share each other's content and support each other's marketing goals. Two heads are always better than one and sometimes getting input from other people can lead you to important insights you wouldn't otherwise have access to.

Apart from sharing information and insight, communication with other pages can be maintained with the aim of directly assisting each other. Perhaps a portion of someone else's followers could potentially be interested in what you have to offer, or vice-versa. These kinds of collaborations between pages and brands are fairly common on Facebook and beyond. Although it's not the only way to go about it, looking to those brands and managers who operate within similar waters as you do will usually yield better results. If you are selling cars, for example, there may not be much room for cooperation with a restaurant owner, obviously. However, seeking out a business whose trade is related to yours opens up a world of opportunity to help each other out and promote your products to a wider audience, and you will find that many businesses are more than open towards this kind of partnership.

- Connect with community influencers

Influencers are Facebook users who have a lot of followers, are prolific in sharing content and are admired by your target audience. Each niche or industry has its own Facebook influencers. You need to identify these people and reach out to them. Most of them will not share your content just because you ask them to. You also need to identify what sort of content they like to share so you can provide them with content tailored to their interests and sphere of influence. You can create a website article that mentions them, for example. It is common for websites to create articles about bloggers to encourage sharing from the most influential ones. You can create the same type of content on your website and tag each blogger you include, when you share your content on Facebook.

Content providers with a very large follower base may sometimes struggle to meet the demand. Those pages are usually on the lookout for fresh content from prospecting pages that aspire towards increasing their followership. This is where you come in if your content is similar to that of the large page. You can get in contact with them and offer to provide certain content, which they will post and give the due credit to you. It's a win-win agreement; you get promoted by an influential page, allowing you to tap into a huge audience, and the page satisfies their followers with more original content. Always take heed not to be taken advantage of, though, and make sure you are properly credited and mentioned if someone else uses your content.

Some of the community influencers in your area are going to make a big difference in how you will be able to sell your products. Take a look around Facebook and find out who is a top leader in your industry and find ways to connect to them. You don't have to be pushy; you can just leave some comments on the page where it is relevant, answer questions to help out, or do other things that aren't going to be seen as spam on the page but actually bring in some value to the page so that others see that you are a great business person and will check out your page as well.

- Focus the content you share on your chosen topic

Your page should be a clear representation of what your business is about. You can only attract the audience you're hoping to if you post the right kind of content. This has to fit their preferences. If you consistently post content that looks like spam, or isn't focused on what your business does and why it's important to them, your followers will lose interest.

Look to your own experience of using Facebook. When you scroll through your news feed, you don't want it to be oversaturated with posts that don't interest you. And imagine if you liked a certain page because you wanted to get regular updates on the content and services they said they were all about, and then you eventually find that they also post a bunch of other stuff that has nothing to do with what the page was initially about. You would unlike that page, or stop following their posts at the very least. Nobody likes their already busy homepage to be further crowded by useless posts, and Facebook makes it very easy for its users to filter out annoying posts, pages, and people.

There are quite a few business owners who will let their content get out of focus or they will ramble. You should sit down and determine what you would like to sell, the messages that you want to get across to others, and how you want your page to feel. Keep these on hand any time that you post to ensure that you are going to reach your audience and that your message is staying consistent.

Chapter 6: Accomplishing Specific Marketing Goals with Facebook

As we have already covered, Facebook is one of the most powerful platforms for marketing right now. There is an increasing number of useful tools Facebook puts at the disposal of businesses, and these tools can be used to a number of different ends. Taking the nature of the internet and social media into account, it's safe to assume that these tools and services will only get more numerous and effective as time goes by. Apart from drawing interest to your presence on Facebook as a primary goal, Facebook can be of great help if you wish to use it to pull traffic to a different place on the internet, your website, for instance.

There are many goals you can accomplish using Facebook. Facebook ads, for example, optimize your ad placement to help you attain those goals. Here are the different types of leads you can generate using Facebook:

- Page Post engagement – likes, comments and shares of specific posts.

- Page likes – used to increase the reach of your organic posts.

- Clicks through to your website – effective for driving traffic to your website.

- Other forms of website conversion: You can also use Facebook ads to convert visitors from social media to perform specific actions, like signing up for a newsletter, or accessing your services.

Facebook's website conversion tool is easy to use. It allows you to track all sorts of user actions, including leads, unique page views, users adding to a shopping basket (including those who abandon the cart before checking out) and registrations. Once you've decided and indicated which categories you'll be using, Facebook provides you with a piece of code. This is called a "conversion pixel". Cut and paste this code into the URL of any pages you'd like tracked and you're there.

This tool can be used to track user actions on any websites you manage. In case you have someone else managing a certain website, you can arrange for them to receive the code as well. Facebook provides an option for this when you are setting up your website conversion. Simply choose this option and you will be able to email the snipped of code to that person directly from the screen. Whatever your chosen system may be, all that's left is to go back to the conversion tool and observe the results under the conversion tracking tab. You will be shown whatever information you wish to keep track of and have a clear picture of how many checkouts, registrations, sign ups, etc. the users on your site are performing.

You can also use the conversion pixel to build your own ad on Facebook. As we've mentioned already, these you'll have to pay for. It's up to you to decide whether your page's development has reached the point at which you're willing to spend money to promote your product or service. You can start with one of the lower cost options, to test the effectiveness of using the strategy. Starting small and building is always the best way to test for impact.

Paid ads are an almost guaranteed boost, but their effectiveness may be greater if your page has already been developed past a certain level. It's about the return on your investment. These ads will almost always help, but you want them to help as much as possible since you're paying for them. It's best to lay down a solid foundation first and accumulate a considerable following on your page before beginning to invest monetarily into your marketing efforts. Either way, there is still going to be some diligence required on your part when creating the ads. There is some caution to be exercised if you are to direct your adverts towards the people of utmost potential for conversion.

By carefully selecting from the variety of demographic markers offered (age, location, gender, etc.), you get more bang for your buck, by getting your ad in front of the eyes of people you know are going to find what you have to offer of interest.

Choose your budget and the duration of the ad and you're done. Learning to use Facebook advertisements is a great way to extend the reach of your page and also, create conversions that result in sales for your business.

- Apps installation and engagement: You can also create ads to make people interact with, download and sign up for your app. Having an app further consolidates your brand and strengthens its name, but it's important to know how to attract people to actually download and use it. In addition to making the app useful for your customers, you can always promote it through your ads.

- Event responses and Promotional offers: If you are a local business and you have promotions and events coming up, you can use Facebook to reach your target audience to make sure that your promotion is successful by setting up an event page. This can be shared with a variety of groups in your community, including those of specific interest to your target audience. There may be new followers and customers in any one of these groups and events can be a rich source of new business.

- Video views: If your marketing strategy is heavily reliant on videos, then you can jumpstart a video's popularity by promoting it through Facebook ads.

- Local awareness: This goal refers to encouraging people to go to your brick and mortar store. By posting ads with this as the call to action, Facebook will provide directions to your store whenever users click on your ad's call-to-action button. If they don't know where you are, how can they shop there?

Increasing Sales Numbers through Facebook

For most e-commerce websites, the bottom line is to increase sales. Here are some proven methods to improve your sales numbers, using organic and paid methods on Facebook:

- Post specific promotions to your page

If you have promotions coming up, you can encourage people to buy from your online and brick-and-mortar stores by posting about the promotion you're running on your Facebook page. You can boost the post to increase its reach and encourage engagement as the date of the promotion approaches.

Your customers always want to get a good deal when they are shopping with you so if you are doing a promotion, make sure that the customers know about it. When you post these promotions on your Facebook page, you will be able to convince them to make another purchase, especially if they were on the fence about making that purchase in the first place. In addition, seeing that promotion could give someone the incentive to check out your page and fall in love with the products.

- Create ads targeted to people who have visited your website before

Facebook ads have excellent targeting algorithms. Aside from employing a user's personal information to accurately target ads, you can also use a person's past behavior. This includes past search queries and website visits. This is the reason your page is targeted by specific Amazon product ads, right after you've browsed Amazon.

You will be able to set up something that is similar. The algorithm will be able to find out when someone has been on your page and then when they get on their Facebook account, they will start to see some ads from your company and some of the different products that are available. This helps to keep your company at the top of their mind and may even show them a new product that they would be interested in purchasing as well.

- Build your relationship with loyal customers and create promotions especially for them

As stated earlier in this book, you can create deeper relationships with your customers by using closed Facebook groups. You can reward these loyal customers by creating promotions specifically for them. You can start contests that only they can enter. You can also provide small gifts specifically for them. By creating a value-added feature, you create a community of people who will discuss your product or service and also need it. People enjoy exclusivity and being part of something a little special. Making your customers and followers feel special is a way to grow your reputation and your client base.

You can also use contests to further promote your product line and expand your audience. It's simple, really. All you have to do is set up a contest where people enter by sharing your post, for example. That's killing two birds with one stone; your followers are participating in a contest for a valuable prize, thus getting more engaged with your page and brand, but they are also promoting your business at the same time. You can also set up your contests in a way that requires the participants to visit your website outside of Facebook and register there, sign up for your newsletter, or download your app. If your giveaway prize is valuable, people will do it, rest assured.

- Recommend items using referral links to create a passive income stream

If your page is considered a source of reliable information by your followers, then you can make passive income by sharing your pages with reviews of items and services your target audience may become interested in. These pages should contain banner ads and text links with referral codes. Once your followers click through these ads or text links and complete a purchase, you will get a commission for your effort.

The more followers you have, the more influence, and thus you will get more opportunities to partner up with various other businesses who may want to pay solid money for you to promote their products in this manner. This is also called affiliate marketing and is one of the most popular methods of earning passive income among bloggers, website managers, and owners of successful Facebook pages.

- Add a "shop now" call to action to your page

If your page gets a lot of visits, then you can also encourage visitors to go to your website by adding a "shop now" call to action to your Facebook page. This call-to-action button should lead to a landing page that encourages visitors to take action. For instance, you can lead your visitors to a page that shows the best deals offered at both your online and brick-and-mortar outlets.

Adding a shop now call to action on your page is going to make a big difference to how well the customer is going to receive your product. They will be able to feel a sense of urgency when it comes to whether they will be able to make the purchase. They will see what they are supposed to do and then they will make the purchase right away rather than waiting.

- Create content that encourages purchases and share them on Facebook

You should create content for people who are in the later stages of the buying process. These include reviews about the products you sell, recommendations based on your products and services, and special offers that may give your followers discounts, targeted specifically to them. By telling your followers the story of how your product or service has had a positive impact on your clientele, you're inviting them to the party. You're showing them why they need it and leading them by the hand to the sale.

After creating the content, you need to make sure it reaches the right people. You can share it on Facebook and boost the post by targeting people who are interested in the product and who reside in areas from which your store is readily accessible.

- Encourage buyers to give a positive review in your Facebook page

If your Facebook page describes you as a local business, Facebook will add a business review feature on the side of the page. People will be able to rate their business transactions with you on a 5-star scale. They may also add a description of their experience. Your goal is to get a lot of 5 start reviews. The problem is that most satisfied customers will not go back to your page to add a review. You need to encourage them to do this by providing excellent customer service and following up on their transaction experience. A direct ask, at point of purchase, is the best way to solicit positive reviews. Develop a script to assist you and your staff in making this a part of every transaction that takes place. It might read something like this:

"Thanks for shopping with us. If you're happy with your experience, we'd love for you to share that happiness with our other followers and customers and spread the love". Cheerful, positive and collegial is the tone you want to achieve. The message can be adapted to a note that appears at the conclusion of online purchases, also.

You can also use reviews left on your Facebook page, or in person reviews (with the permission of the client, of course) as testimonials on your website. People are more comfortable buying products and services that have positive reviews. In a world of slipshod business practices, positive reviews demonstrate your trustworthiness and the quality you offer. There's nothing more compelling than a glowing recommendation and nothing more likely to convert Facebook followers into sales. Positive reviews are one of the most effective tools in your toolbox.

On the other hand, nothing sticks out of the crowd like a one-star review. A negative review can be so powerful that it even discredits the multiple positive ones that may have come before it. When potential customers see a positive review, it's great; it encourages them to do business with you, and that's where it usually ends. But, when they see very negative feedback, they will want to know why it was given; they will look into it if they wanted to buy your product or service. Unfortunately, such feedback often speaks much louder than positive reviews, which is due to the fact that people are generally cautious with the way they spend their money, especially if they are not familiar with your brand. Of course, there's only one sure way to avoid getting one-star reviews, and that's going the extra mile to ensure your products and customer service are on a high level. So, never neglect to pay attention to the reviews people leave as they can make or break a brand, especially if it's only starting to make a name for itself.

More on Passive Income

Your Facebook page is not only a support to your existing business. It can bring you additional income. By using your Facebook page as a springboard for an easy to manage online business, in addition to your existing one, you create a reliable and low maintenance revenue stream that will stand you in good stood when the going gets tough.

Here's something else traditional business has right — diversifying your revenue stream is the surest way to survive in business. If your business is strong, you may think the day won't come that you'll need the support of another source of cash. That would be the wrong thing to think. The world of business is volatile and unpredictable. Today's consumer class has a short attention span and plenty of distractions in the market. Don't be caught short. Create another revenue stream.

Before we entertain some examples, let's look at what passive income actually means. The term itself is nothing new. As opposed to active sources of income, which are regular forms of employment most people take up, passive income represents a source of revenue that just sort of sits there, bringing in money almost autonomously. Think real estate, for example; you own an office space or apartment that you rent out to a certain client, which means you are producing income without putting in any concrete work. That's passive income

93

by definition. The same applies to making a deposit in a bank and cashing in on the interest rates every year, again, making money without any work.

Of course, some sources of passive income will require some work here and there, but they are usually low maintenance and require very little attention. If a passive income source does require you to put in work, though, it will be while you are setting up the operation. If that's the case, it's okay because it's all about putting in the work sooner so that you don't have to later.

With the proliferation of the internet, many new forms of passive income have popped up – and continue to pop up – all over the place. More and more people are choosing to set up their own sources of money online rather than work long hours or multiple jobs just to make ends meet. But, many of them also turn towards the internet just to make something extra without much effort. Either way, the opportunities to make money online are becoming increasingly widespread and available to all. It has gotten to the point where online sources of passive income can replace regular work as a means of making a living, and they do.

It's important to be creative if you wish to set up a source of passive income. If you have a hobby that entails the creation of anything from pieces of art to videos, the chances are that you can capitalize on that through the internet if you look in the right places. If perhaps, you have certain knowledge or a skill that may be useful to others, you can find websites where you can set up courses in a given field and make money off that. Consider the talents you may have and do your research; you'll find that the internet provides countless ways of profiting off those talents.

The best part about the vast majority of passive income sources online is that they require no initial investment money-wise, just creativity and a little dose of ingenuity.

A great example is Teespring. With absolutely no investment on your part, you can make passive income by tapping into cultural trends that can be easily expressed on a simple t-shirt. All you do is come up with the slogan and design.

The simplicity of some t-shirt designs that have seen unprecedented popularity is incredible. People sometimes get crazed about the simplest and most trivial things. Arguably, one can come up with a successful idea with little to no talent in this field. Imagine what you can do if you already possess talent in design and drawing, for example.

If you're already creating some of your own visual content for Facebook (which I strongly advise you learn to do, if you haven't already), creating a t-shirt is a cinch. The tricky part is creating one with a message that has the potential to go viral.

Your imagination is key. But that won't be a problem for a creative entrepreneur like you.

Using Facebook ads (that cost as little as $10), you can test your idea. Before doing that, though, you should be putting it in front of a trusted community, especially if that community is plugged into cultural trends. That might be your family, friends, or colleagues. If it looks like a go from the feedback you receive, $10 is a small investment for the potential returns.

Ten bucks is a small amount to waste, and it is a completely negligible amount to invest into something that may pay off hundreds of times over. It is a proven method too, trialed and tested by those who have seen great success in this area.

Online t-shirt entrepreneur, Marc Boulos, returned a $175,000 profit with his low maintenance enterprise in only one year. The secret, he says, is that $10 ad. If you believe you have a good idea, this ad will tell you if you're right. Boulos targeted veterans, graduating high school seniors and even people with Irish surnames for St. Patrick's Day.

Apart from t-shirts and Teespring, there is a wide range of websites that engage in very similar business. Some of the more prominent sites offer many products other than just t-shirts as well. These are places where anybody can sign up, come up with a design or a piece of art and upload it to be sold on t-shirts, mugs, laptop skins, phone cases, prints, notebook covers, and a lot of other merchandise. The way these sites usually operate is by producing the goods and selling them while giving you a percentage cut of the price since you provided the design. If your print really takes off, these percentages can yield quite a profit, as you've read just above. The takeoff is where advertising such as Facebook ads comes into play to boost your business venture.

There are endless ways you can create a passive revenue stream and endless ideas floating around in your head that you can let out to play on Facebook. So much more than just a secondary marketing tool, Facebook can be your field of dreams.

The only limit is your imagination and your entrepreneurial spirit.

Passive Income through Affiliate Marketing

On a more general note, venturing further than just Facebook for a minute, let us explore the idea of online passive income even further through one of the more popular ways of achieving it, specifically through marketing.

Just earlier in this chapter, we made a mention of something called affiliate marketing. This happens to be one of the most prominent and easiest ways of earning passive income online. Affiliate marketing is the most popular among bloggers, website and page managers, content creators on YouTube and similar sites based on original content, and others. What this means, fundamentally, is promoting someone else's products or services on your platform, advertising them to your followers, and making income through commissions or previously agreed upon fixed rates on each sale conversion that takes place as a result of the ads you host. The deal doesn't have to be about getting paid only when a sale takes place, though. Certain merchants and websites will offer a commission or payment for specific actions that the people you direct through ads will take on their websites. For example, you can arrange an affiliate marketing partnership in a way where you get paid every time someone clicks somewhere, registers or signs up for a newsletter on the site you advertise. This is especially common when advertising a website that isn't really selling anything but is just looking to increase its traffic.

The larger of a following you have, the more you can leverage it to get some rather lucrative deals from various brands, small and big. Basically, this means that someone else will ride the wave of the success of your website or page to draw more attention to their own business. But remember, your power is in your followership. Never forget that without the traffic you enjoy on your platform, you would lose it all.

This is one of the main ways that bloggers, for example, make their living. When their blog reaches a considerable following, and they grow more influential, they usually begin to look for such opportunities. Rarely will you find a big blogger who does it just as a hobby and without making any money off it.

Now, while affiliate marketing sounds like a foolproof way of making money at first, there is more to it, including some risks. Namely, you have to be very careful with what you market to your audience for a number of reasons.

It can take quite a while to amass a big following on your page, website, or blog, and all of that effort and success can go to waste if you take a wrong turn with ads. Keep in mind that advertisements are a very sensitive racket, and don't forget that the majority of people, by default, simply don't like adds. The products, services or websites that you choose to promote to your audience should ideally relate to your content in some way. If you force people to shuffle through ads that have nothing to do with the content they come to you for, they will quickly become annoyed with you. This can drive many followers, even loyal ones, away from your business and severely damage your brand. Furthermore, ad-blocking browser extensions are a popular tool, and your platform will soon find itself blocked for ads if you push it too far, regardless of how much good will the users may have had before.

So, stay away from businesses that have nothing to do with your niche and, once again, avoid promoting sensitive things. As we have already covered, those are religious affiliations, political campaigns, groups focused on sensitive social issues, etc. If you have a very loyal followership, you will be able to push it to a certain extent, but exercise extreme caution, respect your audience and their time and cherish the relationship you have built with them.

If you have a very large audience, you will be afforded more choice at who you partner up with. The best thing to do is seek out a service or product line that is similar to yours or, even better, one that directly connects to yours. For example, say you own a successful bookstore, or you run a blog about works of literature. You can then promote a service within a similar domain, the likes of which would be Audible, a successful audiobook store owned by Amazon. I have personally encountered this many times on the internet. I have seen some of my favorite content creators partner up with Amazon and promote Audible's business, as well as their promotions where they offer a free audio book to all those who register. This is a great example of how affiliate marketing should be done. It's beneficial to absolutely every party involved; you make passive income, your followers get a free audio book, and Audible promotes its services to your audience – an all-around win-win.

Another thing worth mentioning is that you can increase revenue by simply asking your followers to make your page or website an exception if they are using an ad blocking extension. Ad blockers are one of the biggest enemies of marketing online, and they do a really thorough job of blocking out all advertising. You may think that it's too straightforward or demanding to ask people to allow ads when they browse through your content, but it really isn't. Many websites do that, and people do meet them halfway if the relationship is right. The problem is that many users are so accustomed to blocking ads that they simply don't even think about it anymore. For them, it's likely to be no big deal to whitelist your platform, and for you, it can mean a lot.

Although offers for affiliate marketing can often come on their own once your platform grows past a certain point, you can still get in contact with businesses and websites on your own initiative. Either way, affiliate marketing is a very good way of making money and, as I've said, people make a full living off it with great success, Facebook page managers included.

The appeal of such a way to make money is not only in the money earned, but it's also in the fact that affiliate marketing is an epitome of online passive income. All you have to do is set up the marketing agreement, go back to tending to your audience or customer base, and just let the money trickle in. If it can work as a primary source of income, it can work even better as an additional venture to make some money on the side, giving you the security of always having something to fall back on. As far as sources of passive income go, affiliate marketing is as passive as it gets.

The nice thing about this option is that you are actually able to sit back and let someone else do the work in this case. Many people mistake what passive income is in other cases. They assume they can sit back and never do any work, but you usually have to do something. Working in real estate is considered passive income, but unless you have built up a big empire of buildings and have someone to check on them for you all the time, you are going to have to put in the work. The stock market is considered a passive source of income, but again, you will need to go through and watch the market, make switches in what you are doing with your money and so on.

But when you are working with affiliate marketing, you are truly allowing someone else to do the work. These people are going to work to promote your product in some way for you. Those who participate in affiliate marketing are going to advertise, post the advertisements on their websites, and more, so that you are able to sit back and watch the money come in. You will be responsible for giving the affiliate marketer a bit of the profits that you make, but since you don't really need to do the work in the process, you are going to see some amazing results.

You need to make sure that you are writing out a good agreement that someone else is going to want to work on with you. It isn't going to do you much good to only offer a bit of profit for the affiliate marketer on each product they sell. They are looking to make an income as well so make sure that your agreement is fair and that you are giving them a good incentive to really sell the product well.

Chapter 7: Using facebook live to reach your marketing goals

Another neat tool that you are able to use when marketing on Facebook is Facebook Live. Facebook Live may sound like a simple video service, one that offers live streaming, but you will be able to use it in so many of the different marketing tasks that you want to do. Don't mistake this simply for something that records your message and then you never touch again. You can use it to promote events, to interact with the messages and comments that are coming in while you stream, and so much more. It is going to make a big difference in your Facebook marketing and can ensure that you are providing the right interaction with your customers.

On the surface, you will notice that Facebook Live is basically a feature that you can use on Facebook that will allow you to do a live stream video. Pretty much anyone is able to do it and even many who don't use it for marketing purposes have given it a try. But as a marketing tool, this is one of the easiest, plus smartest, ways that you can interact with customers.

With this feature, you will be able to tap on the live stream icon on your page, broadcast your message, whether it is short or long, and then write a description down about the event. Any of your followers will be able to tune in to the broadcast, just like they might do when turning on the news in the afternoon. You can then tap the finish button when you are done with the video.

There are several nice things that you will be able to do with this. First, you get to interact with your customers, sharing news, information, and more right when they need to know it. You can look at the comments as you go, answering questions if some of the customers have them. In addition, Facebook will take the live video and post it on your timeline, allowing followers who weren't available for the livestream to still see the information without you having to do any work with this.

You will need to let your followers know that you plan to do a live stream though. While a few of them may be online if you randomly post a livestream, you will get better results a few days in advance. Simply posting on your timeline about the livestream or setting up a group reminder can really help to make sure that as many people as possible are able to get in on the live video.

As of right now, there is a limit for the broadcast to be under 30 minutes, so try to keep the information or the broadcast below this amount of time. If you need to extend it, you can create a few videos and put them up to continue broadcasting live, but this does give a bit of a choppy look to the video. You also have the option of choosing who gets to watch the video and blocking people if they seem to put negative comments down or they are rude to some of your other followers.

At first glance, you may think that this feature is pretty similar to some of the other live streaming products that are on the market, including Meerkat and Periscope. However, you will find that there are some big differences that come with Facebook Live and the more you use the product, the more these differences are going to come out. Two of the most notable differences with this app compared to some of the others is that Facebook Live is able to retrieve the videos that you need at any time and it works well with some of the other Facebook apps.

When it comes to Facebook, you are always going to get the very best and while there are a few other great live streaming options that you can go with, none of them are going to have all the features and benefits that you will be able to use when it comes to using Facebook Live. Give it a try for your business and see what a difference it is going to make.

There are a lot of different things that you will be able to do when you choose Facebook Live. Not only is this an easy program that allows you to broadcast live to your customers, something that is not always available with other video programs, you get to choose the length of the broadcast as well as what you are going to do while the camera is rolling.

The important part here is to remember that you need to catch your customers' attention as well as work to really provide them with something of value. Sitting beside the camera and just talking for twenty minutes can get boring pretty quickly. Facebook Live is an interactive format so one of the best things to do is talk for a few minutes and then answer the questions and comments that you are receiving by others who are listening to you. This is a basic question and answer segment that many businesses will do on occasion to get familiar with how Facebook Live works and how they will be able to use it in the future.

That is not the only thing that you are able to do with this program though. You need to make it interesting, especially since the most successful way to use this program is to use it often rather than just once. Have a sweepstakes going on, find a creative way to share your message, or do something else that will really grab the attention of your audience and ensures that they are getting some valuable information, as well as some entertainment, out o what you are doing.

One last thing, if you are using Facebook Live, make sure that you are giving some announcements about when you will be broadcasting live. Sure, this will post the recording on your Facebook business page when you are done, but the most value for your customers will come if they are able to catch the podcasts live. Announce the times that you will go live at least a few days ahead of time so that your customers have time to see the announcements and can go on and watch you. If you plan on working on this app each week, make the time the same (at least as much as possible) so that your customers know when to expect the next live stream.

HOW TO USE FACEBOOK LIVE

Now that we have taken some time to look at Facebook Live, it is time to look at some of the ways that you will be able to use this feature to market your products. Just from the little introduction that was above, you probably already have a few ideas of ways that you can broadcast for your business. For example, you may choose to live stream an announcement for your company, show some interviews, or even have a seminar that your customers would enjoy.

It is all going to depend on the angle that you want to take with your business and how the live streaming is going to be able to benefit you the most. Some of the things that you should keep in mind when it comes to using Facebook Live for your business includes:

- Attract more followers—anyone who follows you on Facebook is going to receive a notification when you go live with a broadcast. You should make sure that these people are going to check out your livestream, whether they do it right when you go live or at a later time when they can get to it, by providing high quality experiences, rather than just wasting up airspace.

- Tell them in advance—you can do as many of these livestream events as you want, but if you don't tell people about the live event, you are going to have a hard time getting anyone to watch it. You should make at least one announcement, although several are the best, so that the followers know that you are going live at a particular time and even announce what you will be talking about.

- Check the connection—nothing is worse than going through all the hassle of creating a live broadcast and getting all your followers to show up than to find out that the Wi-Fi doesn't work. Make sure that you check the reliability and speed of your connection and that everything is in good working order so the live stream keeps going well the whole time.

- Write a good headline—you should provide the viewer with some information about the stream so that they have the right information to know whether they want to watch it or not. You should make the description engaging and interesting so that you can compel others to participate.

- Engage with the viewers—show your appreciation for the viewers coming in and watching the show and attract some new ones by engaging with them. Ask for any feedback that others have, respond to their questions, and aim to make the experience more participatory rather than a big long lecture.

- Do longer broadcasts—if you only have time for a shorter broadcast on occasion, that is fine, but do consider having some longer ones on occasion. This will make it easier to answer the questions that your customers have and to really interact with them in a new and exciting way. You can choose the length that is right for you, but if you want to give your customers a chance to interact and have fun with you, going for longer periods is important.
- Go live often—the most effective way to use Facebook Live is to do these often. You don't need to do one each day, but having a livestream each week or so, keeping interaction with your customers and answering their questions or concerns, can really make a difference. You may want to consider setting it for the same time each week so that your followers can be prepared to watch it and you won't have to remind them quite as much.
- Be creative—no one wants to watch a boring livestream. You need to make sure that you are putting up interesting content, not just posting in the hopes of getting more customers. Have a purpose behind your

livestreams, rather than just having the camera rolling. Think of giveaways that you can do, fun contests, and easy things that you can do in order to bring in the customers and make them feel like they are getting some benefit from watching your show. If you are able to come up with an idea that is out of the box and really creative, it is a good idea to give it a try; you never know when it is going to appeal to your customers and can give you the results that you need.

Facebook Live is a great program that you will be able to use in order to reach your customers in a more interactive and caring way. No matter what kind of business you are, if you are already using Facebook to help promote, you will find that adding in some Facebook Live on occasion will make a big difference.

BENEFITS OF USING FACEBOOK LIVE FOR YOUR BUSINESS

There are many benefits that you are going to receive when you choose to have Facebook Live for your business. This is an easy tool that allows you to get instant contact with your customers, in real time, no matter where you are located on the planet. Some of the benefits that you may like when using Facebook Live for your business include:

- Able to interact with customers—this is one of the best ways to interact with customers. You can answer their questions, show them new products, and explain a big event that is coming up. This is much more personal compared to working with just writing or doing a press release so you are going to get a better review from others.

- Answer questions in real time—your customers are bound to have some questions in regards to your products and the things that you are selling. You will be able to answer these questions in real time. Some people find that it is easiest to talk a bit about a new product or event and then read through the comments for any questions or concerns that the customers have. Other times you may ask your customers to ask questions ahead of time and then you are able to answer these questions in the livestream when you start the recording.

- Easy to use—Facebook live is a great option because it is really easy to use. If you have a Facebook page for your business, you will be able to use Facebook Live. You simply need to go onto the app and then click the record button. And then until you are all done, the app is going to record you. You will be able to add in a description for your viewers, look at comments, and pretty much respond in any way that you would like.

- Adds more freedom for creativity—when you are able to use video, especially live video, you are going to find that your options of being creative when reaching your customers. The sky is the limit as long as you use the streaming in the proper way. You can have contests, answer questions, throw a big party, celebrate some of the new followers who are on your page, and so much more than ever before.

Using Facebook Live is a great addition to your marketing campaign. You simply need to find out where it is on your Facebook page, announce any of the live events that you are going to do, and take the time to come up with some creative options that will help you to interact with the customers and keep them interested in the work that you are doing. It doesn't matter what kind of product or service you are using you will be able to find that Facebook Live is a great tool to help you out.

Chapter 8: Other Cool tools that you can use with facebook marketing

This guidebook has spent a lot of time looking at some of the best marketing tools that you will be able to use to make your business stand out from the crowd. While there are a lot of different marketing techniques that you can use, Facebook is one of the most versatile and allows you to reach your consumer in ways that you couldn't before. Some of the other cool tools that you are able to use when it comes to using Facebook for your marketing plan include:

AGORA PULSE

The first tool that we will use is the Agora Pulse. This is a dashboard that you are able to use on Facebook, as well as Twitter if you are moving your campaign over there as well. This will basically show you an overview of all the activity that goes on with your page and can make it easy to schedule posts and even to begin that campaign right from your dashboards. There are a ton of campaign types that you are able to use when it comes to Agora Pulse including:

- Sweepstakes
- Quiz
- Personality test

- Instant win
- Fan vote
- Coupon
- Photo contest

You will be able to pick one of these to use and then you can add on any of the information that you need for the campaign. You can then promote this campaign using a simple post on your page like you would with any of the other information that you are sending to your customers. There is going to be a cap on the amount of participants that you are able to use if you go with the free version, but if you go with one of the paid plans (which starts at $29 a month), you will be able to lit up this cap.

EDGERANK CHECKER

This is a program that is owned by Social Bakers, but it is one of the best social media sites that you can use when it comes to taking a look at your Facebook page. It is going to provide charts and graphs for you to see how your page is doing and to get a more in depth look at what is going on when it comes to the amount of views, who is visiting your page, and so much more.

If you are on the free version, you are going to be able to take a look at the graphs and the charts. But if you would like to learn a bit more about your visitors and get some in depth information about your page, it is a good idea to go with the paid plans. They will provide some of those key metrics and page recommendations that you need to make the best decisions for your business.

SHORTSTACK

This is one of the most comprehensive campaign tools to use with Facebook and it is going to make it pretty easy to add on any campaign that you would like. In fact, you may be surprised about the amount of options that you are able to use when it comes to making a campaign on your page. You will be able to use some of the templates that come from the page or you can go from scratch and make your own campaign using the intuitive visual editor.

ShortStack is going to be a great because if you already have the ideas ready for a campaign you can make it go live in just a few minutes. Even if you are just getting started, you will find that you can get the campaign up and running in no time. There is a simple plan that is free and can work with your Facebook account, or you can get some more advanced options and upgrade to the paid plan.

FACEBOOK PAGE BAROMETER

Sometimes it is nice to get an overall look at the health of your page. You will be able to use the Facebook page barometer to determine how your page is working on its own as well as how it is doing when compared to some of the other pages that are of the same scale and size. This is another tool that you are able to use from Agora Pulse if you use the advanced features on there and you can look at various statistics including virality, feedback, engagement, and reach. Once you have this information, you will be able to compare it to the results of pages that are similar in terms of the amount of fans.

This tool is going to breakdown your page based on the amount of views that you have, so that you are able to see what is going on with your particular group. Some of the benchmarks that you can look at include:

- Under 10000
- 1,000 to 10,000
- 10,000 to 50,000
- 50,000 to 100,000
- Over 100,000

AGORAPULSE CONTEST

A great way for you to entice the customers to choose your page over another one is to do a contest. You can have your customers participate in a certain way, such as liking and sharing your page or doing another fun activity, in order to win a prize. There is a lot that you can do with the contests to make it stand out from others and you can choose the contest that works out the best for your particular product.

The AgoraPulse contest gives you a lot of fun things that you are able to do. it has lots of options in terms of the contest that you are able to pick and the parameters that you can set around it. Some of the contests that are available through this app include:

- Sweepstakes—the sweepstakes will do a lot of the work for you because they will randomly pick out winners from among the fans who either commented or liked, or some other way reacted, to your post.
- Quiz—you can set up a question or a small quiz that you would like your customers to answer. You will then get a smaller pool of people who answered correctly and you can pick a winner from there.
- Photo contest—with this one, you will be able to ask some of your fans to comment with a photo. You will be

able to pick out a winner from the one that has the most likes at the end of the contest period.

A bonus that you are able to do with this app is that you can store the winners in the program for later. This makes it easier to refer back to later if you want to make sure that the same person isn't winning each time.

LIKEALYZER

If you are new to Facebook marketing, you may want to consider going with the LIkealyzer tool. This one is going to help give you some suggestions when it comes to how to improve your page. You will be able to use this tool in order to review your Facebook pages, as many of them as you would like. Then the program will take the time to provide you with an overall score for the page as well as gives you some recommendations on where you should improve your score.

All that you must do in order to get this program to work is enter the URL for the Facebook page that you would like to use. The nice thing is that this app will not need to authorize with Facebook before doing the work. Once the URL is in place, Likealyzer will take a look at the page and will then return blocks o easy to read data as well as some advice on how to improve the health of your page so you can really star to interact with your customers more.

WOLFRAM ALPHA PERSONAL ANALYTICS

While we have spent some time talking about a few apps that you are able to use that analyze your page, this is one of the best ones that you can use. This one is great because it really goes into details for profile pages and personal brands and can provide you some more details than what you will be able to see with some of your other options. Keep in mind that while this one goes into more details than you will find with some of the other options, you will not be able to use it with business pages, only with personal pages or profile pages.

There is going to be a lot of information that you are able to get when you put in your personal or profile page. Some of the information that will come up with this app includes:

- Most liked posts
- Word cloud and word frequency
- Post lengths
- Post statistics
- Weekly post distribution
- Types of activity that is going on between you and your followers such as statuses, photos, and links.

This can all come together to give you a pretty good idea of how you are doing on the page and what you may need to improve on. Most of the time there are going to be some areas you are doing well in and others that you need to make some improvements with. When you start to use this type of analytics, you are going to see that it is easier than ever to see what is going on.

One of the best things that you can do is get some insights into the friends who are following you and the ones who are actually seeing your posts and making comments. Some of the insights that you are able to see about your followers and which can really help you to move those to focus on them include:

- Network map
- Friend locations as well as their local times
- Ages as well as their youngest and oldest friends
- Relationship status placed into a pie chart
- Gender split

POSTPLANNER

PostpPlanner is an app that is meant to help you to get more views. They have claims that state how they are able to triple your engagement in just a few minutes each day. They have one case study on their website that claims that they were able to get almost three million views on a post. This post came from a page that only had 59,000 fans. So how did this happen. The key with this is the viral search feature that is found on PostPlanner's page.

To use this feature, you are going to need to search for the most viral content that is on Facebook and then reshare it, or post it, on your own timeline. You can even schedule what time that you would like to have these new posting come up on your page so that you hit as many of your followers as possible.

The main plans with PostPlanner come in at $29, but there are a few apps through Facebook that you are able to try out that are for free so that you can give it a try and see how it works for you.

PAGEMODO

If you would like to have a bit more freedom over your business page and want to create something that is completely yours, Pagemodo is the best option to go with. this one is going to allow you to find content, schedule posts, design a more visual post than before, design your cover image, run some contests, and even create some new Facebook tabs are that are custom.

The cover creation is a great tool to use to help set your page apart from some of the others. You will be given the dimensions that you are able to use through Pagemodo and then you can fill in and also arrange out the photos that you would like to do. You can use the same steps when it comes to your visual posts because you will be able to fill in any of the content that you want to be customer, choose a template, and you can even use Pagemodo to help you post directly to Facebook.

The more features you would like to use with this the more it is going to cost. There are some free versions that are available and will give you time to get your feet wet and to try it out. If you want to have some more features or some more freedom with this app, you will find that the plans are pretty affordable and start out at just $3 a month.

As you can see, there are many apps that you are able to use when it comes to working with Facebook. This is one of the biggest social media sites around and it has been in use for many years now. Because it is so popular, you will find that a lot of people want to post on it to share with their customers and make their business grow. You will find there are a ton of great apps that you are able to use in order to make your business page stand out and to increase your reach and your sales.

Chapter 9 : The latest marketing trends with facebook

Working on Facebook is a great way to reach your target audience and to ensure they are gaining the message that you want them to. But with that being said, you need to keep up with all the latest trends that are going on around you. There are many other businesses who are also using Facebook as a way to market themselves and with so many products available, it is no wonder that it is harder than ever to reach your target audience.

But despite all this competition, Facebook is still one of the best online marketing techniques that you can use. You should consider getting well-versed in some of these great marketing trends if you would like to make sure that your page is standing out from the crowd and that you are actually bringing in some of the clients that you want.

COMPETITION IS HIGHER THAN EVER

For those who have never used Facebook to market before, you need to be aware that the competition is so much fiercer than ever before. There are over 1.59 billion users on Facebook at this time and the number is always growing. This is a huge target audience that you are able to tap into and even if you won't need most of those people to purchase your product, it is a great place to start. In addition, there was over $17 billion spent on Facebook advertising in 2015 and the number is already growing in 2016.

Since the amount of advertisers as well as personal profiles are growing on Facebook, the competition as well as the bid prices on the ad action continue to rise. More advertisers want to get a piece of the pie so it is always becoming more expensive to work on Facebook. This is especially true when it comes to mobile advertising with Facebook. It is important to note that while Google is still the biggest advertising platform online in terms of revenue, Facebook's ad revenue grow by 48.6 percent while Google only grew by 13% in 2015.

The trend continues to grow for Facebook. While $17 billion is a large number, it is really only about 3 percent of all the ad spending throughout the world. Since Facebook has a lot of options for you to choose from and you can measure the results better than with other options, it is likely that more advertising budget is going to shift over there. In fact there are already many companies that are already shifting their televisions over to Facebook as well as Instagram because they are able to reach bigger audiences and can increase the amount of sales that are used.

What this means for you is that there is going to be a lot of competition that comes in when using Facebook. Many businesses are starting to see the value in using this option and they want to be able to reach their target audience as well as possible But there is still a lot of room to grow since there are so many users on this platform. If you are smart with your advertising budget and can learn how to stick out from the crowd, you will see that this is still an efficient way to increase your reach as well as your sales for an affordable price.

MOBILE IS KING OF THE RING

When you want to reach your customers on Facebook, you need to make sure that you are advertising on the mobile phone. Facebook is growing to include many mobile friendly options and even Google has started to penalize websites that are not friendly for mobile devices. One new feature with Facebook is that the new ad formats are going to work on the computer, but they are mainly optimized to work on mobile devices.

As technology grows, many of your customers are relying more and more on their mobile phones. They take these phones wherever they are going, to work, to school, to the grocery store, and they use them all the time. Because of this, if you want to be able to reach your customers, you need to have your advertisements work well on the mobile phone.

If you find that your website looks bad or doesn't work that well on a mobile phone, you are going to lose a lot of your conversion rate. The amount that is spent on mobile advertising has grown in 2016 and it is finally bigger than desktop ad spending for the first time ever.

USING DYNAMIC RETARGETING

One thing that you should consider with your Facebook advertising is dynamic retargeting. This is a new ad strategy that is going to let you personalize your ad so that ever impression is going to feature products or other content that was recently viewed or has some relevance to the user.

These are mostly going to be done in static ads so you will not have an ad that changes around while the viewer is looking. This one is going to pull out information from the users product feeds, such as product names, prices, and product images, and then will feature this content in their adds. The ad creatives are going to be dynamic, since the ad can often change based on what the user puts inside.

Basically, this kind of advertising is going to take a look at what your customer is viewing or shopping for, and then find a way to make this meet up with the product that works for them. This makes the ads more personal and in fact, you will see that your click rates can double and triple from this compared to the traditional static ads.

UPSELLINGA ND CROSS-SELLING

Cross-selling is a really useful way to increase the value of your customer. When using this option, you will take a look at the product that the customer picked and then you can show them other items that are related. While the customer may not need the same product again, say a handbag, they may be interested in some accessories or some shoes to complete an outfit or another project that is somehow related to the first. When you suggest these products, you could end up selling some extra products compared to just selling the one.

Upselling is another way to make more money from the customer, especially if you are just able to get them to purchase one thing. Say that your customer picked out a handbag that they like. Before they check out, you can set up the system to show a few other products, other handbags that are similar or would provide a value in another way, that may cost a few dollars more. These may entice the customer to go for the higher priced product because they perceive some kind of value with it. They provide a higher profit margin to you, but still provide the same benefits that the customer is looking for.

You will be able to do both of these processes with Facebook using the Dynamic Product Ads. In fact, Facebook is going to automatically do all of this from you based on the product sets that you are showing in ads. It will then decide which products should be shown based on what the customer picked using many techniques. For example, if you have a lot of customers who purchase rings and necklaces together, this Facebook feature is going to learn to offer necklaces each time your customer purchases a ring.

STANDING OUT FROM THE CROWD

The important part of picking out new software to use in your advertising in Facebook is to find the right mix that is going to help you to stand out from the crowd and makes your product look better than all of the others that are out there. What works the best with another company is not necessarily going to work the best when you put it towards your products. We have talked about many different types of products and services that you are able to use on Facebook, but you are the one who is responsible for figuring out what is going to work out the best to target your audience as well as to push forward your products.

The best thing that you can do is use the latest in the targeting options that are available. Facebook is always changing and adding on more tools that you are able to use in order to propel your business forward and you will be able to use any and all of them to help market your products. This is true no matter what kind of marketing tool you are trying to use. They are always adapting and trying to reach customers in the best way, and if you are able to keep up with this, you are going to find that you are able to reach your customers in ways that you never have.

Not only are you responsible for picking out the right marketing tools to use with Facebook for your product, but you also need to make sure that you are using these marketing tools in the best ways possible. It doesn't do you any good to get the information from your data retrieval sites if you never look at the data and it doesn't do you any good to use Facebook Live just to talk for two minutes just once rather than doing something that is creative and going to capture the attention of your target audience.

You need to know how to use the tools that you want for your product. You need to be creative, learn how to use tools like Facebook Live and the different sweepstakes and so on that are available. If you don't know how to use them already, you either need to learn how to use them or consider avoiding these in the first place. While the tools can be really nice to use, it is better to avoid them and go with ones that you know rather than ruin your reputation and turn away customers going with tools that you don't know how to use.

Facebook is one of the best tools that you will be able to use in order to promote your business and get customers in the door. It has a broad reach to others in your customer base and will ensure that you are able to reach as many people as possible. The trick with using this option is to learn how each of the tools work and use them in the most creative way possible while enticing customers and helping them to see that your product is one of the best that they can choose. The tools that are presented in this guidebook will help you to get ahead when it comes to reaching your target audience on Facebook so you can interact with the right customers while also seeing your profits rise.

Conclusion

Thank you again for downloading this book!

I hope I was able to help you reach your marketing goals using Facebook.

As you have seen, this form of marketing allows opportunities traditionally beyond the reach of regular advertising. Hopefully, you have learned one of two things; either how to grow your Facebook page and successfully promote your own business on the website or how to cash in on your success and turn your followership into a source of passive income as well, wherever that audience may be gathered on the internet.

The best thing about Facebook and the Internet, in general, is the fact that most business ventures you want to try yourself in require little to no financial investment, especially in the beginning. And as the internet and social media engrave themselves even deeper into our everyday lives and develop even further in the future, these opportunities are bound to become only more accessible to all.

The vast majority of users on the website use Facebook every day without even thinking about the business potential that's right in front of them the whole time. But, those who run a business have generally realized the importance of social media, and you will find that even the smallest of businesses have their Facebook pages nowadays. While it's true that a lot of those pages don't grow that much, this is not something that's beyond their control. The difference between them and you is that they are not well-informed, unfortunately, and simply lack the knowhow to take their page to new heights. Hopefully, now you possess enough of that information to make yourself stand out from the crowd.

The next step is to continue to create and share content that your followers love and to build relationships that may convert to future sales. Keep this book handy when implementing your Facebook marketing strategies and come back to it every time you feel a little lost in the Facebook marketing world.

Remember to keep evolving your relationship with your customers and followers and remain in touch with their requirements and interests. A business that cherishes their relationship with the clients is the healthiest and most solid in the long run, and Facebook has facilitated the building of such a relationship like no platform has done ever before.

If we continue down this road, then perhaps television and print will continue to decline in popularity, if not become completely pushed aside by the internet and social media. We could very well be on the ground floor of something completely new. We could see a time when social media becomes so prevalent throughout the world that the very concept of media changes dramatically and evolves into something else entirely.

Think back to a time when television was just starting to become more popular and accessible for a moment. Television forever revolutionized media, but at first, it gave a voice only to a select few people, like the state or big businesses and those who they would give the floor to from time to time. Nowadays, with social media, virtually anybody with an internet connection has the potential to reach millions, if not billions of people throughout the world. This allows us to share ideas and advanced knowledge with such ease, let alone share and promote a line of products or a service. Influence and power are now measured by views, followers, and visitor traffic. Even if an audience is all you have going for your page, once you achieve a large one, you will instantly be faced with numerous opportunities and new roads to take, letting you choose the direction you want to take with your business.

www.ingramcontent.com/pod-product-compliance
Lightning Source LLC
Chambersburg PA
CBHW030526210326
41597CB00013B/1045